MINDING A
SACRED PLACE

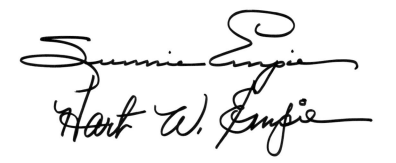

MINDING A SACRED PLACE

By Sunnie Empie

Photography by Hart W. Empie

BOULDER HOUSE PUBLISHERS
Scottsdale, Arizona
2001

Minding a Sacred Place
Copyright © 2001 by Sunnie Empie and Hart W. Empie
First published in the United States of America by
BOULDER HOUSE PUBLISHERS

Library of Congress Cataloging-in-Publication Data
Empie, Sunnie (Arlene Sundquist), 1932-
    Minding a sacred place / by Sunnie Empie; photography by Hart W. Empie.—1st ed.
        p. cm.
    Includes bibliographical references and index.
    ISBN 1-931025-03-7
    1. Boulder House (Ariz.) 2. Johnson, Charles F. (Charles Foreman) 3. Architecture,
Domestic—Arizona. 4. Organic architecture—Arizona. 5. Architecture, Modern—20th
century—Arizona. 6. Empie Petroglyph Site (Ariz.) 7. Indians of North
America—Arizona—History. I. Empie, Hart W., 1926 – II. Title.

    NA7235.A6 E48 2001
    728'.372'092—dc21   00-050728

Book and jacket design by: David Alcorn
Printed by: CS Graphics, Singapore
Published in the United States of America

FIRST EDITION

10 9 8 7 6 5 4 3 2 1

Western diamondback rattlesnakes, *Crotalus atrox,* mating.

Endpapers: Lichens growing on the Precambrian granitic stone.

Contents

Provocative prehistoric rock imagery and natural architecture meet in a magnificent outcrop of Precambrian boulders in the high Sonoran Desert.

A Sense of Place

Desert Mystique
A Spirit of Place

The majestic saguaro, *Cereus giganteus,* is the trademark of the Sonoran Desert. It may take seventy-five years before a saguaro grows its first arm, and at full maturity of 150-200 years, it can be fifty feet tall and weigh as much as eight to ten tons.

Preceding pages: The spectacular formation rises dramatically from the flat desert terrain to dominate the landscape with its presence—a towering, jumbled mass of Precambrian boulders that covers almost an acre of land.

"**M**UST SELL MY BEAUTIFUL PILE OF BOULDERS NEAR CAREFREE, ARIZONA," read the August 1974 advertisement in *The Carefree Enterprise*, a small community newsmagazine. The caption was an eye catcher to Hart W. (Bill) Empie, a third-generation Arizonan who has an affinity for the high country of the Sonoran Desert. I share his enthusiasm for open spaces. Bill's Arizona beginnings are in his blood memory, and he longed to return. His father, Augustus W. Empie, was born in Arizona Territory before statehood, and Bill was born in Safford, Arizona. For him, the call of the desert was loud and clear.

We were living in Olympia, Washington, at the time Bill discovered the ad. We frequently visited Arizona's Sonoran Desert, not only as a respite from western Washington's excessive number of gray days, but more for the spiritual catharsis the desert offered. I needed little encouragement when Bill suggested that we take a look at the "beautiful pile of boulders" in Arizona. Even though my roots are in the Puget Sound region of Washington State, the wet weather was cause for periodic angst. I was not averse to experiencing life in an arid desert climate, and in fact, the idea was quite tantalizing.

Within days, we were on our way to take our first look at the boulders. With a sense of adventure in the air and the seller's instructions in hand, we drove north on Scottsdale Road into the foothills to find the old trail that the seller had described as "two ruts through the desert." His note read, "About a hundred yards past a rustic, carved wood cactus-identification sign with 'Prickly Pear' painted in white letters." The property wasn't in the city of Scottsdale then, as it is now. It was "way out there" in the country.

Meandering eastward on the narrow road through pristine desert, past towering saguaros, ironwood, palo verde, and gnarly old mesquite trees, we thought about the people who had passed this way before us. Over 12,000 years ago, Paleo-Indians crossed central Arizona as they followed the migratory paths of large animals such as mammoths and bison. As the climate shifted and large animals were no longer plentiful, the Clovis hunting culture gave way to sparse, semi-nomadic populations of Archaic hunters and gatherers. People living in the Southwest continued to pursue a hunting and gathering way of life until about the first century, when they began to integrate the cultivation of domestic crops such as corn and beans that were introduced from Mesoamerica. There were others: The Hisatsinom, ancient ancestors of the Hopi people, and the Hohokam, who abandoned their sites in the fourteenth century. Throughout the foothills, there are hundreds of ancient sites identified by a scattering of stones from the walls or rock foundations of dwellings, rock alignments, lithic tools, and the remains of broken pottery containers from as early as the first century.

Military and stagecoach roads followed the ancient trails throughout the territory that led to excellent springs. In 1870, the U.S. Army cleared a wagon road through the hills to link Fort McDowell northeast of Phoenix with Fort Whipple near Prescott, the command post for the Arizona Territory. That road opened the foothills to settlers and speculators. The first mining claim was staked in 1873, and then came sheep and cattle ranchers. Nearby Cave Creek, one of Arizona's oldest towns, had its beginnings as a mail stop in 1877 and still exudes a free and pioneering spirit. The land is imbued with human history which, along with the wildness of the landscape, makes up the spirit of place. A spirit of place can get under one's skin. Some call it desert mystique.

We bumped along the narrow trail that was barely visible but still passable—an old road that now belonged to the desert. It was August. The sky was intensely blue, punctuated by thunderheads building on the horizon. The air was heavy and still. Doves rocked gently on the branches of an ocotillo. Occasionally, a startled lizard scurried out of sight over the crushed granite desert floor, and a covey of

The verdant landscape botanically defined as the Arizona Uplands subdivision of the Sonoran Desertscrub. Tall columnar saguaro cacti, *Cereus giganteus,* dominate the landscape. Pinnacle Peak is silhouetted in the background.

Harris' Hawk, *Parabuteo unicinctus,* watches for small prey from its perch high atop the unripened fruit of the saguaro.

A mule deer, *Odocoileus hemionus,* visits the waterhole. Water for the desert's denizens was promised the dowser who used a forked branch from a greasewood bush to find the only place where there was water—815 feet deep.

quail rose in a frightening cloud of chatter from their hiding place in the chaparral. The lush landscape was scattered with granite boulders of various sizes.

In the distance, we finally caught sight of the enormous outcrop of boulders thrusting upward from the relatively flat desert terrain. It was beautiful, but this was no mere "pile of boulders." The spectacular congregation of stone dominated the landscape with its majestic presence. An awesome sight and, certainly, far beyond our expectations as to what we would encounter on our desert adventure. The jumbled mass of stone covered nearly an acre of land and included some monoliths that towered as high as a four-story building.

We stopped the car. Without a spoken word, Bill and I knew that we had found our special place.

We sensed that our introduction to the boulders was a defining moment, as tears blurred our vision. We stood together quietly among the stone monoliths, looking out over the verdant, high Sonoran Desert. There are places in the wild where one is able to experience the earth as it must have felt and looked before the dawn of humans. This is one of those places. Time stood still. In that moment, our presence was gripped by a realization of the past and present merging. It would be rare for us to experience Nature in any form and come away unmoved, but the emotions that surfaced were indeed quite startling. Had we known anything at the time about sacred sites, we might have understood our strong emotional reaction, as well as our shared feeling of coming home. If we were ever to rely on our intuition, this was a time when we recognized place. Feeling a strong sense

of union, we silently shared the beauty and the spirit of the surroundings. We honor that magic presence, that intelligence that directs us unerringly to persons, places, and conditions at the time they are needed.

The property is located at the edge of the desert where the foothills end and the land breaks into the open, gradually descending for miles toward the arid valley below. It is captivatingly beautiful. This is no Lawrence of Arabia desert. The verdant landscape, botanically defined as Arizona Uplands subdivision of the Sonoran Desertscrub, displays a wide diversity of flora that provides sustenance and shelter to a host of desert wildlife: collared peccaries, bobcat, deer, coyotes, reptilians, and rabbits. The graceful, undulating land is lush with desert shrubs and

The bobcat, *Felis rufus*, a high Sonoran Desert predator, rests at the waterhole.

magnificent native trees. Mesquite, palo verde, and ironwood trees nestle within arroyos; and tall saguaro cacti dominate the low ridges, their graceful arms raised upward as they preside over the vast desert.

The upper Sonoran Desert is exclusively home to many indigenous species from the tiniest bird, the phainopepla (Phainopepla nitens), whose survival depends on the desert mistletoe that grows in palo verde trees, to the towering saguaro. Seasonal rainfall in the foothills doubles that of the valley, averaging over sixteen inches annually, which accounts for dense vegetation that the locals may call a "desert forest." In addition to indigenous trees and saguaro cacti, there are cholla, barrel, and hedgehog cacti. Crucifixion-thorn, graythorn, creosote and catclaw bushes are complemented by low shrubs called bur sage—not what one would expect in an arid desert, but this is "high desert."

The collared peccary or javelina, *Pecari tajacu*, has a coat of coarse, grizzled hair. Families travel together and stop at the waterhole. Unfortunately, they are legally hunted in Arizona.

On the hottest of summer days in the desert foothills of central Arizona, we wound our way through the boulders and were awed by the monoliths towering above us. Each time we rounded a massive boulder or peered through a crevice in the stone, another magnificent desert vista appeared before us. The boulders themselves are uncommonly, hauntingly beautiful. The tumbled clusters of granitic stones have rested in silent repose upon the earth, and each other, since Precambrian time, the oldest division of geologic time. The rock outcroppings are about 1.45 billion years old and are found in a narrow belt that continues northwestwardly across central Arizona. The boulders' curvilinear forms were

Black-tailed Jack Rabbit, *Lepus californicus.*

The high Sonoran Desert landscape. In the foreground, chain-fruit cholla cactus, *Opuntia fulgida*.

Following pages: Cactus wrens, *Campylorhynchus brunneicapillus*, refurbish their nest amidst the ripening fruit of a saguaro cactus.

created by a weathering process called exfoliation, whereby small bits of stone gradually sloughed off over the millennia, leaving around us a desert floor carpeted with particles of granite. The natural erosion of the stone surface bestows a texture and softness upon the boulders—words not generally associated with the word "granite." The imposing forms have a tonality and a painterly quality, the colors ranging from warm buff to the charcoal black of desert varnish, with highlights of a reddish-earth shade that we call terra rosa, and a sprinkling of mica. At night, under the light of a full moon, the granite boulders take on a luminescent quality. An eerie glow emanates from this sleeping stone giant.

The contemplation of stone can offer a particular solace. At the same time, however, these enormous boulders exude a magnificent power that summons forth

Above: Chain-fruit cholla cactus, *Opuntia fulgida*, sometimes twelve feet high, creates a remarkable display when laden with fruit clusters. The long, branched chains become heavy and drop, and a new plant is born from the fallen fruit.

Left: The blossom of the saguaro cactus, *Cereus giganteus*, is the state flower of Arizona.

emotions of the past—distant pasts—that gently moisten our eyes. Under the great dome of the open sky, Bill leaned against a boulder to relax for a moment, his lower back pressed firmly against the stone. The massive force that emanated from this living matter startled him, and he called for me to experience the energy. I, too, placed my back against the boulder. The stone giant had only appeared to be sleeping. My encounter with the earth's forces was truly shocking. The energy from the boulders entered my body and swirled in my solar plexus as if I were plugged into an electrical socket by an invisible cord. The force was of such a magnitude and oddity that I sprang away from the boulder wall in disbelief from this intimate discovery that the earth is truly alive.

Preceding pages: The presence of the twenty-foot-high monolith and a single protuberance that appears as a thumb prompted its name—God's hand.

Shiny, black male Phainopepla, *Phainopepla nitens*, and his mate.

Three young great horned owls, *Bubo virginianus,* blend into their stone habitat.

It is the outer layer of these beautiful boulders that commands our attention, but it is their inner energy that is as powerful, positive, and uplifting as the physical appearance of the stones themselves. They reach out to us and radiate warmth from the sun. Walk away from the enormous outcrop of stone and it will be ten degrees cooler down by the dry wash where, over the millennia, runoff rainwater has carved a meandering path around sculptural bedrock boulders. It rains infrequently in the desert, but when it does, it is brief and intense. Water collects and charges through the normally dry desert washes with great force.

Gambel's or desert quail, *Lophortyx gambelii*. A striking topknot of dark feathers identifies this expressive bird.

◎

After we purchased the land, we visited frequently and during those times, we could be found at our special place, picnicking, walking in the desert, or just lazing on a flat boulder, enjoying the warmth of the Arizona sun and the all-encompassing silence that one finds in the wild. The only sound we heard during the night besides coyotes was the occasional strum of automobile tires crossing the old cattle guard on north Scottsdale Road. The metal strips hummed like a stroked guitar in the stillness of a desert night. These were memorable moments. In a short time, a bond was created between persons and place—a sense of place that time nor events can ever erase.

It was, and still is, a place where one can look across a desert morning and hear the animals talking. With the first light of dawn, something arises— something in the air. The yip of a young pup followed by the howl of a coyote, and then plaintive howls—first one pack and then another join the chorus that rings out over the vast expanse of desert. Voices rise, saluting the dawn of a new day. A squirrel sounds a warning to its offspring before the coyote is visible to us. Hawks, ravens, and owls proudly show off their new families as we all watch the young ones fly awkwardly from boulder to saguaro. We observe a quail parent loudly and actively instruct his new covey on how to take a dust bath while he creates a dish-like place in the ground. Then, the tiny quail, no bigger than a thumb, move together like a tightly woven blanket to a natural watering place in a bedrock

Gila woodpecker, *Centurus uropygialis*, clings to the skeleton of a saguaro cactus.

boulder. Each day we fill it with fresh water only two fingers deep so the baby quail won't drown.

It is a place where the first brilliant light of the sun appears

19

Curve-billed thrasher,
Toxostoma curvirostre,
feasting on the red, ripened
fruit of the saguaro cactus.

The raucous, repetitive calls of Arizona's state bird, the cactus wren, *Campylorhynchus brunneicapillus*, do not go unnoticed.

boldly on the horizon and brushes across the desert's soft, green blanket of bur sage bushes. The tall outcrop of stone casts its long shadow over the desert like a bow to the new day. Almost as quickly, the sun rises into the redness of the morning sky, and the elongated shadow withdraws back into the boulders. As the earth awakens to the sun's first rays, spider webs dance around a palo verde tree, the silken strands connecting the branches to the ground. The sun highlights the morning dew that clings to the wispy strands, swaying to the rhythm of the break of day—a vertical rainbow with all the colors dancing. The air is pungent with the sweetest perfume from the desert mistletoe, its root firmly attached to the palo verde tree's branch.

We are reminded each time we visit the remains of ancient dwellings through-out the Southwest that the indigenous people always chose the most beautiful spots; therefore, it was conceivable to us that we should discover something on our property to indicate that the first people who wandered about the Southwest had also been attracted to this place. Even the discovery of the smallest bit of broken pottery would give us great satisfaction. From local reports, there were thousands of broken pieces of ancient pottery scattered about the upper Sonoran Desert foothills.

Bill returned to Washington from a trip to Arizona and said, "I have a present for you." I could not contain my enthusiasm. Visions of a gift of elegant contemporary Native American jewelry danced through my head. He opened his clenched fist and presented two small pottery sherds, explaining that he found them near the boulders. Nothing could have delighted me more. I eagerly demanded more of an explanation: "By the boulders on our property? Where? Tell me again."

When we later returned to the boulders, Bill led me to the place where he found the sherds, bent down, and picked up another one. Laughing, I accused him of salting the area to make me happy because I so wished to find something. The discovery, in essence, was a lesson in going beyond looking—to seeing. People who

Red-on-buff Hohokam potsherds found on the site.

hunt for projectile points know that the first arrowhead is the hardest to find. Once we learn what it is we are looking for, the quest becomes easier. And so it was with the potsherds. I found my first one that day, and from then on I rarely saw the sky. My eyes were intent on seeing the next sherd.

A broken bit of prehistoric pottery was indeed only the beginning of the story that would unfold before us.

◎

Above: Gila Monster,
Heloderma suspectum, an
18-24-inch venomous,
heavy-bodied lizard with
bead-like scales.

Left: Chuckwalla,
Sauromalus obesus, a large,
heavy-bodied lizard inhabits
rocky sites.

Creating Natural Architecture

The boulder outcrop as it
appeared before construc-
tion. The twenty-foot-high
cluster of boulders will
become the interior wall of
the living space.

Preceding pages: Twelfth-
century Wukoki Ruin at
Wupatki National Monument,
Arizona, exemplifies building
in harmony with the earth.

A Quest for the Best
Nature's Materials, Space, and Spirit

The "beautiful pile of boulders" had appeared to us in the *Carefree Enterprise*, an Arizona newsmagazine. Now it seemed that another small ad in *New Mexico* magazine, featuring a new home designed by Charles F. Johnson, would lead us to our designer. "Johnson brings to New Mexico architecture dramatic concepts in timeless design which synthesize the fundamentals of Pueblo Architecture with the basic human needs," the article read. "A grandeur is born that grows from its site."

It was the name of the house, "Anasazi," that first caught Bill's eye. Anasazi, a name adapted by archaeologists to identify one of the early cultural groups in the Southwest, was a familiar name from our research of historic architecture, pottery, and basketry, but it was Johnson's architectural drawing that was compelling—a curvilinear design enhanced by features found in the Southwest's earliest dwellings.

Our requisites for a home in the Southwest were few, but they were important to us. We specifically wanted a sense of the old ancestral Pueblo style of architecture that combines Nature's materials, space, and spirit. We are enamored with the ancient architecture, not only for the spirit that remains, but also for the indigenous materials that the people used for their dwellings and the manner in which the structure itself was integrated into the landscape. At Wupatki National Monument in northern Arizona, for example, the land is a vast, wind-swept, high desert, devoid of trees and seemingly devoid of any structures. Remnants of the dwellings constructed by the Southwest's early people, however, are sequestered at the edge of arroyos or canyons or beside rock outcroppings. They stand apart from each other—much like the desert's plants and trees—allowing space for each other to survive.

Under the overhanging boulder will be the entry into the living space.

These ancient dwellings stand for us as models of buildings that were designed to be at one with the setting. They rise unobtrusively out of the landscape to harmonize with the surroundings and appear as a natural outgrowth of the earth itself. It is difficult to see the demarcation between bedrock boulder and the human-made stone structure. Walls of stone, precisely bound together with little or no mud mortar, now stand open to the sky centuries after the occupants abandoned the sites. Sometimes, the weathered timbers that once supported an ancient mud roof are still in place. We seek out the smaller, isolated ruins, away from the crowd that engulfs the more prominent remains of structures, such as Wupatki, for which the National Monument was named. Although some ruins are only remnants of former structures, the spirit of place is still recognizable. If we stand quietly, we might hear voices still rising and falling with the waves of wind that sweep across the tall, dried grass.

Santa Clara Pueblo Indian Rina Swentzell wrote, "With the belief that places also are alive, Pueblo people visit the old ruins to breathe in the strength of the place and of those who have gone on before."

We also look upon the form and void of the remains of decayed dwellings as sculpture in its natural setting. There is an interplay of conflicting elements in the shape of old ruins: the leaning walls sometimes create an opposing tension, and openings that once were windows and ceilings become the void. The eminent sculptor Henry Moore, whose large abstract bronzes adorn landscapes as well as museums, echoes our own feelings. "When buildings become ruins, they become sculpture," he says. It may be difficult even for us to comprehend where our romance with antiquity comes from, but somewhere deep within our psyche lies the determinants for the choices we make, including the manner in which we choose to live. That quality we call beauty grows out of our experiences.

It was the ancient structures that came to mind as we began to think about our new home in a desert setting. When we place a building on this earth, it must not only be responsive to the site, but also the materials must be ecologically responsible and in harmony with the environment. The architecture, in essence, must be a composition of Nature's materials, space, and spirit. The small drawing of Johnson's that we saw in *New Mexico* magazine was enough to suggest that perhaps here was a person who understood the nuances of the historic Southwest architecture and who could translate our dream of a home in the desert into reality.

◎

With Johnson in mind as a possible architect, we went to Santa Fe where a realtor graciously showed us the house featured in the ad, along with two others. Johnson's architecture seemed to grow out of the earth with adobe walls up to two feet thick. Sunlight and shadow moved across the interior walls and highlighted the undulating curves of the hand-plastered adobe walls. The fluid quality of the curvilinear designs unfolded into a succession of graceful, open living spaces.

The boulders before construction.

Following pages: The figure is standing where the stairs will be, and the boulders on the facing page will be incorporated into the guest room.

Passageways curved and opened to new visual experiences. As in Nature, there were no rectilinear shapes nor ninety-degree angles in Johnson's houses. We felt relaxed and embraced by shelter. An open floor plan and his use of space pushed the boundaries of the definition of rooms. The homes appeared more as habitable artforms than residences.

We were exhilarated by our discovery of the historic regional precedent coming together in Johnson's contemporary Southwest architecture. He clearly was familiar with the features the ancestral Puebloans incorporated in the first buildings constructed in the Southwest in the eleventh century. The wood lintels over the windows, for example, were laid on the ledges of sculptural buttresses that were wider at the base and curved upward to the ceiling. Peeled pine logs supported the

roof. The ancient builders used ceiling timbers to support the weight of their mud-plastered roofs, and the timbers were used over and over again as buildings were renovated. Timber was a limited resource, so they were never cut to fit the dimension of a new room, which is why we see the supporting timbers extended outward beyond the walls at varying lengths. Between the timbers, small saplings were placed at right angles, and then the roof was finished with a dense layer of packed earth. There are fine examples of centuries-old buildings at Taos and San Ildefonso Pueblos that are still inhabited.

After our Santa Fe excursion, we sent Johnson photos of our enormous outcrop of boulders and the surrounding land. "What would you think of doing a house in Arizona?" we asked. He was astonished by the size of the boulders when he first saw the photo of Bill leaning against them, dwarfed by the standing stones, and was prompted, unbeknownst to us, to travel to Arizona to see our site. He climbed upward through a jumbled mass of stone and walked into a vast space that was almost enclosed within thirty-foot-high boulders, one cluster measuring ninety-five feet long. Johnson sensed they were much too powerful and would overwhelm any dwelling he might build beside them. He later told us that as he stood within the enormous outcrop, he was struck with the thought that the boulders were themselves the natural house on the site: Why not let the site become the house? Why not build the house of the boulders, among the boulders, and within the boulders?

Johnson's response arrived a few weeks later, and in the packet was a conceptual drawing of a house as he had imagined. The drawing was accompanied by a straightforward letter in which he wrote, "To do other than build within the enormous pile of boulders would be grim." His idea astonished us. We had not considered such a possibility. The gigantic cluster of boulders near the center of ten beautiful acres of pristine desert land was the focal point and the center of our activities while we were on the site, but small outcroppings nearby would be enchanting building sites, and a tree-lined arroyo meandering east to west through the property presented more opportunities. We hadn't really picked a favorite spot. We wrote back to Johnson and told him that the concept drawing "blew our minds," as was the expression of the 1970s, and that we would like to meet with him.

Johnson saw the possibility of a window in the diamond-shape opening below the balanced boulder.

Johnson's proposal that more than sixty percent of the walls of our home would be natural weathered granite was out of the ordinary, but with the framework of existing boulders and his explanation about tying together those spaces that had a domestic scale, we could visualize living within an outcrop of stone. I was completing a design program at The Evergreen State College, and so I had some sense of spatial organization to intelligently evaluate the situation. Also, Bill had years of creative experience in the advertising display business. Indeed, we were both captivated by Johnson's bold notion, and the thought of interviewing anyone else vanished from our minds. But why this immediate acceptance of something as unfamiliar as living within boulders? Or was it unfamiliar?

Living closely with Nature was not a new experience to us. I grew up on a farm in Washington State, and I spent hours outdoors in the fields and gardens helping with planting, harvesting and farm chores. The land was alive with the

sounds of birds and insects. From the porch of the farmhouse, the aroma of warm wood and freshly mown grass permeated the air. Bill, a third-generation Arizonan, has a keen sense of place. When he was three years old, his parents lived on the Apache Reservation. Bill's moccasined feet followed his Apache nanny, Inez, along the same paths at Old San Carlos that the Apaches walked for centuries. It was 1929, and his father, Gus, was employed as timekeeper for the Coolidge Dam project. The majority of the workers were Apaches, and his daily contact with them developed into kinship as well as mutual admiration. The original Old San Carlos village is now under Coolidge Lake behind the dam, but in Bill's memory is a family experience enhanced by their relationship with the Native Americans and reflected in his quiet, gentle manner,

Triangular windows are set into the stone above and below the concrete lintel that also encircles the base of the balanced boulder.

his ability to walk softly, and his sense of the land. Bill also recalls that as a boy, he played near the ancient Hohokam Casa Grande ruins at Coolidge, Arizona, and walked the desert barefoot. A desert he remembers as being soft and resilient. He and his boyhood friends dug a cave deep into the earth and a tunneled passageway through which small desert Elf Owls would glide.

We met Charles Johnson poolside at Camelback Inn in Scottsdale in the spring of 1978 amid a desert setting punctuated by brilliant spring blossoms and felt immediately at ease with this friendly person with an affable smile. We laughed about coincidences: Bill and I had gone to New Mexico to view his architecture without telling him; Johnson had traveled to Arizona to get a glimpse of our site without informing us. We finally met. He told us about his design background. He had received his bachelor of architecture degree from the University of Southern California and had been designing residences in the West since 1954. With a spellbinding enthusiasm for architecture, his voice rose and matched our own excitement as he described how he would use the natural boulders as walls and passage-ways within our home.

We were gratified to learn that his philosophy of architectural design is derived from that of Frank Lloyd Wright. Although he never studied under Wright, Johnson's architecture is rooted in the American tradition of "organic architecture" as defined by Wright (1867-1959) and Bruce Goff (1904-82), both of whom he admired. Their design philosophy places great emphasis on environmental sensitivity. In Wright's view, the structure, its appointments, and its setting all are integrated. He believes that the natural elements of the site—its materials, topography, and climate—are not only major considerations but should inspire the design of a building.

Johnson explained to us his own process of design: He will visit a site many times to study contours, views, wind, sun, trees, neighbors, and he studies the client's lifestyle. "Architecture is really about people," he told us. "It's about designing experiences that enhance the awareness and enjoyment of living life." He explained that after learning about our lifestyle, he would address each space relative to how it would be used to enhance our *experience* of living that particular activity. He considers each of his designs a "collection of experiences" that takes his client far beyond function into the psychological aspects of experience. For example, he told us that "cooking is an art form, and the surrounding space should not only function well, but be pleasant, stimulating, and complementary to the experience."

Johnson's seemingly simple request that we think about how we lived prompted thoughts far beyond the question, *How* do we live? We asked ourselves: *Why* do we live the way we do? *What* brings us to build our nest in the manner in which we do? People have an innate will toward shelter, which is among the most basic of human needs. And to a child, shelter is a space in which to play. Left to their imagination, creativity blossoms in the form of a tree house and the cave at the beach with driftwood walls and a weathered plank door. Or for some children, a house scaled to their size constructed of clapboard painted red with white trim and a planter box of geraniums in the window.

The questions transported me back to my first experiences of shelter. My thoughts reentered the warmth and security of the imposing farmhouse that my grandfather built and where I lived as a child. I recalled a warm and cozy shelter that I created by the wood stove in the kitchen of that house when I was five years old. Soft light filtered through a worn, cotton flannel sheet that enveloped a small table. Emotions resurfaced as I recalled how I felt when a game warden arrived

looking for signs of pheasant that he thought my father had poached out of season. The warden tore away the exterior of my "house" in his search for evidence of feathers.

There also was a tree house under a spreading juniper tree—its arms creating an umbrella-like canopy twenty feet or more. Covered with a thick layer of needles, the earth was like a soft, rust-colored carpet. The aroma of juniper cones permeated the air. The solitude and quiet, the dim light that filtered through thick branches, the coolness on a hot summer day, all remain within my memory.

Johnson continued to probe about our routine domestic activities and where they usually take place. Among the questions: How do you entertain? Where do you usually eat your meals? Where do you dine with guests? Is sunrise a special time of day? Are you night people? Do you share a bed? Do you share a bath? Creating a personal residence means revealing behavior and idiosyncrasies that sometimes even your own family doesn't know. In order to meld client needs with the design of the home, Johnson then asks himself questions and reflects on the experience more than the event. What will the experience be like? What will it be like to dine here—or there? How will sunlight, moonlight, or firelight enhance the experience? All of these questions provoked deep introspection about how we lived and led us to ask ourselves, What did we *really* want?

We referred to our architect-designed home in Olympia, Washington, and described its features and materials indigenous to the area: The interior space felt limitless and flowed uninterrupted throughout the glass and cedar house. Open spaces with lofty ceilings unfolded one after another down the gentle hillside to Ward Lake. Hand-split cedar shakes covered the roof, and handsome, natural clear-cedar exterior siding continued visually uninterrupted onto the interior walls. Vast windows invited the Pacific Northwest's soft light. Tall fir and cedar trees were visible from every room as well as a 20-foot-tall vine maple tree that grew within a glass-enclosed atrium, its branches reaching upward and visible from all three floors. It was the Northwest architect's expression of living in harmony with Nature.

For Johnson, the description of our Washington home and its relationship to its site affirmed for him that we would be receptive to his idea of designing our Southwest home in, around, over, and under boulders. Granted, the arid desert is a vast departure from the cool and rainy Pacific Northwest, but living closely with Nature was something we had always done, and we had the same expectations for our desert dwelling.

We had found a designer with an affinity for natural architecture, and we signed the contract with Charles F. Johnson, poolside, at Camelback Inn 4 April 1978.

Thinking Like a Rock
A Boulder Approach to Architecture

"Design credit for the recently completed house must be given to Nature as well as to Charles Johnson. The character of the house derives, to a large extent, from the character of the boulders—voluminous masses, some tilted, some crevassed, all grained and variously spaced: room for passages, room for rooms. The architect and owners respected and sensed the site; they preserved it. The site remains a mystery, a discovery, an activity—and the central meaning of the Empie home."

— Joseph Giovannini, architectural critic and author,
"Charles Foreman Johnson," *Architectural Digest.*

He threaded his way among the boulders, noting their position as well as the location of five grand palo verde trees sequestered among the boulder outcrop. Preserving the pristine state of the natural rock forms was of primary concern, as the weathered granite would ultimately become the walls of our home. Moving the enormous boulders was never a consideration. There were spaces within the boulders that had a domestic scale he saw as living spaces, while other spaces between boulders suggested passageways. The challenge for Charles F. Johnson was to form living spaces by connecting the boulders in logical places to make the house and Nature become one—without intruding on either the stone or the indigenous trees. His goal was to tie the architecture to the site so that it would appear as if an architectural seed was planted and Nature grew the building.

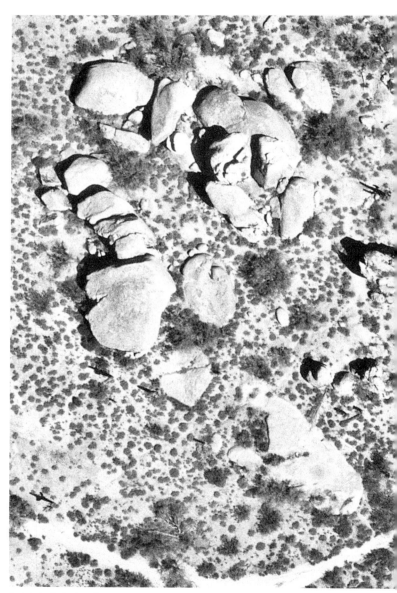

Johnson studied the land's features: contours, views, wind, sun, trees, and most of all, he said, the psychological feeling. For boulders to truly "work" when incorporated within a dwelling, he knew there must be synergy between the creative person and the stone. "I had to get my mind to think like Nature when she creates a boulder," he said, "and then to think like a boulder to understand how Nature goes about doing design. The house will be an extension of Nature, so it's like the rocks suggesting the architecture. You see sunlight entering through crevices and you design a window. By 'thinking like a rock,' I design so the new is compatible and in harmony with the ageless."

Aerial photo by Landiscor.

Generating a Plan

Peeled pine logs (vigas) fan out over the library.

An aerial photo and a topographic map of the site created by field survey and photogrammetric service were tools that helped Johnson determine floor elevations and the locations of constructed walls. The aerial photo shows two clusters of boulders that form an open V-shape. The formation that makes up the natural west wall is about ninety-five feet long, twenty-five feet high, and twenty-five feet wide at the base. The other cluster, that is more loosely defined, would be incorporated into active living spaces. The vast, open space between the two dominant clusters was the obvious choice for the common living area, and the long, west wall would protect the interior from the hot afternoon sun. A problem loomed, however. There were features of the stone that were not visible on the aerial photograph, such as open crevices, fissures, and niches. Furthermore, leaning boulders and peculiar rock overhangs concealed what was beneath, so Johnson had to assess carefully each boulder on site to clarify the configuration of the stone and then consider how it could be incorporated into the design. He was acutely aware that it would be very easy to do something with these rocks and have it go wrong.

Five brass markers were secured on key boulders throughout the site, and the elevations noted. The brass benchmark on the low boulder at the southeast end of the living space reads 2296 feet elevation. From that point, using a transit, a surveyor's instrument, he obtained vertical measurements to determine where the proposed floor levels would intersect with the boulders, and those elevations were then marked on the stone. Johnson took great care to adapt the floor levels to the existing ground elevation aound the boulders so there would be little site excavation.

Buttress that meets the balanced boulder is reinforced with concrete and iron rebar.

Architecture Grows from the Site

Ordinarily, the walls of a house are constructed on top of a poured concrete slab that is the configuration of the floor plan. However, in this case, the boulders would determine the location of the walls, thus they were designed before the floors were poured. Johnson knew that plumb walls would be at odds with the flowing curves of the boulders, so each wall was shaped

The window glass is set into the kerfed stone and the caulking packed with granules of stone so that the boulder continues visually uninterrupted from outside into the interior.

to work visually with the rock. He explained, "When incorporating boulders into a dwelling, or the dwelling into the natural outcrop of boulders, the architectural elements need to flow gracefully and become an extension of the natural surroundings."

To mirror the forms found in Nature, not one wall is straight—rather they curve and undulate to create a compatible relationship with the boulders. The exterior walls are as much as one foot thicker at the base than at the top and lean inward from ground level to parapet at a ratio of one inch per eight feet, meaning an eight-foot-high wall leans inward by eight inches. The walls range from fourteen to twenty inches deep, with the buttresses over four feet at their greatest depth and up

to three feet wide.

First conceptual drawing.

Building a boulder house presented challenges that called for innovative approaches to design and construction. One of those challenges was to inform the workers how to build the entry wall so that it would slant inward to meet the boulder overhead. Johnson instructed the men to place a concrete block on top of the stone to secure the string that slanted to the outside of the footings and then to build the wall on a slant following the string. Beneath the massive boulder leaning over the entry, Johnson designed a narrow stone stairway to give the illusion of climbing confined steps to an ancient Indian ruin. It was rebuilt three times to achieve the effect he wanted. A low, sculptural wall beside the stone steps invites one to look over the edge and down to the base of the towering boulder leaning overhead. Johnson laid out some walls with a garden hose that he adjusted inward or outward to fine-tune the architectural flow, and then he sprayed a line of paint on the ground where the workers dug trenches for the footings. It is not exaggeration to say that walls started to go up and walls came down.

There had been the initial flurry of excitement when we blessed the land in

April 1979 with a gathering of friends and family. However, once we were back in Olympia and creative work began on our site 1500 miles away, it was unclear why Johnson would not share the composition in his mind by sending us copious sketches and drawings. Architecture buffs that we are, we were eager not only to see elevation drawings of the interior, but also to participate in the design process. We mused that the lack of drawings might be because he felt clients simply do not

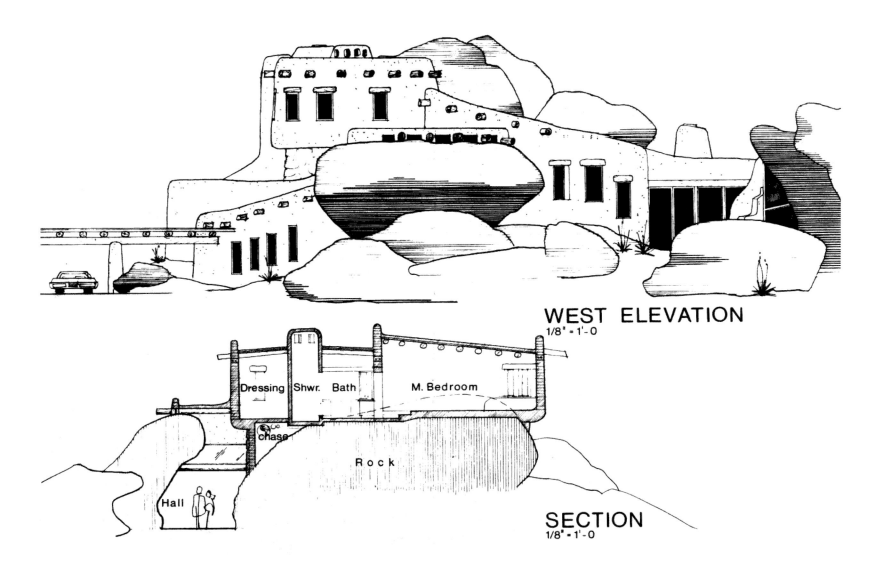

WEST ELEVATION
1/8" = 1'-0

SECTION
1/8" = 1'-0

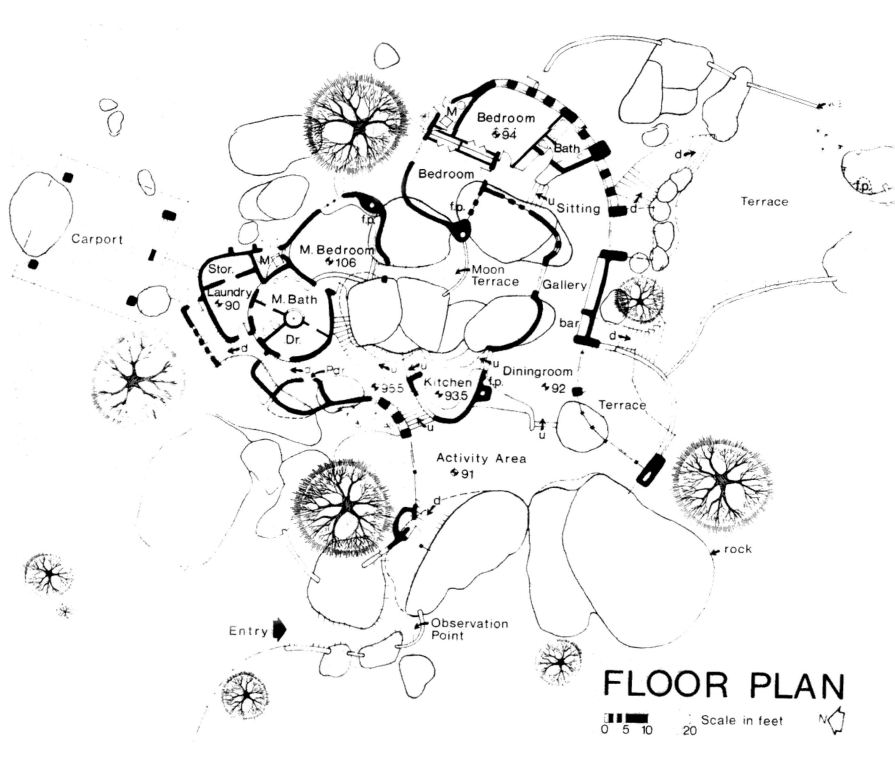

Bedroom
$94
M
Bath
Bedroom
f.p.
u Sitting
d
d
Terrace
f.p.
f.p.
Carport
M. Bedroom
$106
Moon
Terrace
Gallery
Stor.
M
Laundry
$90
M. Bath
bar
d
d
Dr.
u
u
u
Diningroom
$92
d
d Par.
$955
Kitchen
$93.5
f.p.
Terrace
u
u
u
Activity Area
$91
rock
d
Entry
Observation
Point

FLOOR PLAN

Scale in feet
0 5 10   20

N

understand the creative process. Since Johnson is a devotee of Frank Lloyd Wright's work, perhaps studying Wright's modus operandi would help us understand Johnson's design process as well as his arms-length attitude. I read about Wright's work, his behavior and client relationships, and ultimately concluded that he, too, didn't think much of a client's ability to understand architecture. I also gleaned that he was keenly aware of the "limitations of graphic representations."

Edgar Kaufman, Jr. in his book, *Fallingwater*, writes: "Wright might well have agreed with the French philosopher Jean Paul Sartre—a 'quality. . . is given to every moment insofar as I am living in it. . . which it loses when I am living in it no longer.' " It seemed to us that Johnson, too, could not proceed comfortably with himself and with the process unless he was living in it.

Johnson offered his own explanation: Of the residences he had designed, he felt that our house in the boulders was the easiest and fastest to design initially, but it presented the most difficulty in revisions and refinements. It just wasn't the kind of house in which the design evolved from the drafting table. He explained that the floor plan could not be determined until the final elevations were chosen, since irregular faces of the rock would become walls. Then there would be further refining where walls and floors intersected with the stone. It appeared then that the initial drawings submitted to the county building department were preliminary drawings created to obtain building approval. With that, designing the handcrafted house began—on site. Only through vision and then revision during the layout would he finally arrive at the point wherein the concept would come into clear focus and then into physical being.

Johnson informed us that he does not create well under pressure. The next step would occur when the creative urge moves him, and he alone would decide when that happens, not someone else's schedule. He understood that this could be bothersome and unrealistic, but it was essential to his well being in order to create. Johnson wrote, "the final product will be drastically better and well worth any

Built around, over, and under weathered granite boulders, the contemporary desert dwelling appears as if an architectural seed was planted and Nature grew the building.

delays." The problem, as we saw it, concerned a minimum of drawings and required a maximum amount of patience. Yet our faith and trust in this man's ability had not diminished, and we were committed to the design process, as he saw it. As the house began to unfold in, around, over, and under the massive stone, we moved into a motor home beside the boulders to watch its progress and to oversee completion of our home. We greeted each new dawn with excitement and anticipation for what the day might bring.

Pine logs (vigas) up to thirty feet long span the living space to meet Douglas fir beams that rest on a massive, curvilinear structure in the center. The thirteen-foot-long pine log is in place for the fireplace opening. (Center of photo)

A Roof Like a Protective Parasol

Hand-hewn pine logs (vigas) radiate throughout the ceiling like the ribs of a protective umbrella. Johnson incorporated vigas into the design of the house as load-bearing roof supports, but equally important, the exposed vigas would aesthetically tie together various defined living spaces by their continuity from one

space to another throughout the interior. Timbers are exposed in the Southwest's stone and adobe buildings that were here long before the Spanish people arrived in the New World. When the Spaniards came across the Indian villages in the 1500s, they called the people Pueblo, which is the Spanish word for village. Features of the early Pueblo architecture then took on Spanish names: The timbers are called vigas, and the saplings or poles laid between the vigas, latillas.

The positioning of the vigas was critical and called for innovative on-site designing. Some boulders leaned inward, some outward, and there were fissures and open crevices between boulders to be dealt with. The space between each of the vigas had to be visually compatible, and Johnson wanted the ceiling to undulate and conform to the rhythm of the vast boulder walls. The crux of the matter was determining where the holes would be cut in the boulders in order to insert one end of each viga. As he told us, "You can't just shove them around once you drill the holes, so the holes have to be in the right spot to start with."

Above and opposite
Positioning the vigas was
achieved by manipulating
the strings that spanned the
living space at ceiling height
from the boulder wall to
mock beams. Each string
represented a viga.

Opposite the boulder wall, the vigas would rest on eight-by-sixteen-inch Douglas fir beams that span the length of the living space to converge upon a massive sculptural structure that accommodates the living room and dining room fireplaces. On the kitchen side, the cooking center would appear as a large, beehive-style fireplace.

Sometimes, the only way to test an architectural idea is to simply try it out. Johnson directed the carpenter to build a truss of two-by-four lengths of lumber that could be jacked up or down to determine the height of the supporting fir beams. He ran cotton string tight across the face of the boulder wall and then looped crosswise strings that could be moved along the taut string against the boulders. The strings were carried across what would be the ceiling, thrown over the mock beam, and weighted for tension. Each string from the boulder wall to the mock beam represented a viga.

Johnson fashioned an eight-foot length of lumber into an implement similar to a shuffleboard paddle and conducted the orchestration by thrusting the baton-like instrument skyward. First, he adjusted the height of the mock beams to create a slope to the roof that would direct rainwater to wide canales (scuppers). Then he manipulated each string that represented a viga to create the undulating pattern. Johnson gestured as he explained, "If you study this roof, it's sort of like taking your hand and fanning it that way and taking the other hand and fanning it this way. None of the vigas are exactly parallel. They all fan out gradually and that gives the soft feeling to the roof." A longer span in some rooms dictates that the viga must be proportionately wider in diameter, one of the nuances that is often over-looked by builders who attempt to use this vernacular feature in contemporary Southwest architecture.

When the initial cuts were drilled into the stone to create the hole for the viga, I screamed as loudly as the shrill of the jackhammer. My intense emotional reaction even startled me, but I believe Nature embraces all living things, including stone. There must be another way to do this without cutting into the majestic rock, I begged. I imagined a time in the future when inevitably the wood has returned to the earth and those gaping black holes in the stone look out over the land like empty holes in a skeleton's skull. The Southwest's early people carved symbolic images in stone that are still visible centuries later. I ponder how people in the future will perceive the holes in the stone when they become the only visible remains of our presence.

Wood chips flew and freshly exposed pine gleamed in the sunlight as 150 hand-selected logs were peeled by hand with a draw knife. Overhead, cranes moved

the pine logs from the staging area onto the roof and guided each viga into place. Johnson specified one-by-twelve-inch natural redwood planks for the ceiling decking because the wood's varying hues would complement the floor and the boulders. The planks were laid on top of the vigas throughout the house, except for the library and my writing room where four-inch red fir latillas, blackened from a natural flash fire, were laid above the vigas in a herringbone pattern. Some of the burnt bark was partially peeled with an adze.

Terra Rosa Floors

The palette of colors and materials used throughout the house complements the texture and tonality of the weathered granite. The earthy rust color of the floors, which we call terra rosa, mirrors Johnson's choice of redwood planking for ceiling decking. The terra rosa was achieved by adding iron oxide pigment to the wet concrete. The thick concrete mix slowly spread out over the sand-filled frame and touched the boulders like waves gently meeting canyon walls at Lake Powell.

Under the fine craftsmanship of brothers Carl and Warren Wolf, master concrete finishers, the floor took on a luster to rival the gleam of the one-eighth-inch-wide copper strips embedded as expansion joints between the pours of concrete. The boulders cast a subtle reflection on the polished floor not unlike the reflection of stone canyon walls in still water. The colored concrete floors extend beyond the glass doors to the terraces; the effect, then, is that both climate-controlled spaces and outdoor living areas are visually uninterrupted.

Fireplaces as Sculpture

The inspiration for the living room fireplace came from a centuries-old design brought by Basque and Russian sheepherders into the American Southwest. In the shepherd's hut, sheep gathered in front of an open fire while the shepherd spread his bedroll on the ledge above the fireplace, out of the way of the animals. The fireplace in our living space reflects that simple design with its open, floor-level

Seventeenth-century shepherd's kitchen at El Rancho de las Golondrinas in New Mexico. The ledge above the fireplace allowed the shepherd a place to sleep while the sheep huddled in front of the fire.

Right: The sculptural fireplace clings to a massive boulder that juts into the room while both reach upward to meet the vigas (pine logs) that fan out overhead like the spokes of a wheel.

hearth and the wide ledge above, although it was expanded to complement the opposing sixty-foot-long boulder wall. For Johnson, however, a problem ensued that the shepherd did not have to contend with—the county building inspector. The thirteen-foot pine log that runs the length of the fireplace was cause for concern, so Johnson designed a metal plate that protects the underside of the log from a spark. The buttress below the center of the span and the gentle curve of the mantel upward to the ceiling were worked and reworked with thick applications of plaster to achieve the sculptural effect that he wanted.

While many people collect clippings of features to incorporate into their dream home, we had stored away memorable moments inspired by the architecture of old Santa Fe dwellings to recreate in our desert home. The raised fireplace visible beyond the end of our dining table was inspired by a visit to a nineteenth-century adobe home in Santa Fe. We toasted our friends, the Deweys, as the fire cast its light on their hearth three feet above the floor—the perfect height to enjoy a fire while seated at the dining table. In front of a grand fireplace at a Santa Fe resort with friends, Janis and Dennis Lyon,

"The ceiling closes like a canopy over the interior, and in the center, the planking all but meets to create a triangular slit (sky crack!). Then in a sudden stroke of inspiration, the chimney slides through to the heavens—a sexual moment in architecture, underscoring the sensuality of the site."

—Noël Bennett, artist and author of *A Place in the Wild—Gentle Architecture for Fragile, Natural Sites.* Funded by The National Endowment for the Arts.

we watched through the skylight overhead as sparks from the fire drifted upward into the darkness of the night sky. The same effect was achieved by embracing the chimney with glass above the dining table so the night sky is visible.

Johnson created our dining room fireplace by using his hands-on approach to design. The plasterer applied the wet scratch coat, the thick first coat of plaster that is heavy with sand, while Johnson sculpted the form with his bare hands. He added, removed, stroked its massive shape, and then stepped back to look it over. The next day he ordered that it be torn down. Designing began anew, and he continued sculpting until it was just right.

The first fire was built by the plasterers to heat their homemade green chile stew. For lack of a serving spoon, the cook found a scrap of redwood and carved a beautiful ladle. During the winter, the coolness that descends over the high desert at dark invites a warming fire. Bill lays a fire with split wood placed on end in teepee fashion against the back wall of the fireplace. His creative formation radiates heat into the room and uses a minimum of firewood that is available only seasonally when woodsmen are permitted to cut fallen juniper trees in Arizona's high country. It was a reflective moment indeed when we lit our first fire. As the soft, wavering light from the burning logs danced across the textured surface of the stone walls, we thought about the people who sat before their fire in a rock shelter millennia ago and watched the chameleon light against the stone.

It was discovered serendipitously that the fireplace Johnson designed under a rock overhang in the guest room was the exact place of ancient fires. During excavation, the ancient firepit was uncovered, and thus the contemporary fireplace was relocated so that the thick carbon from fires of centuries ago would remain untouched. The carbon stain on the underside of the massive reclining boulder had been hidden by dirt sucked into the cave by the updraft of air created by the outcrop of boulders. In recent years, the final protectors of the cave were desert

"Butterfly Rock" in its natural
setting, and the sculptural
butterfly embedded in the
wall. Inside, the powder
room is nestled between the
V in the rocks.

wood rats who built an enormous midden of desert debris that was a monument to their building talents. Their organic architecture, along with scattered fresh joints of desert cholla cactus, protected them from marauders and also concealed the ancient carbon stain.

Between a Rock and a Hard Place

The house began to look like an artist's palette board as we tried on various tones of exterior paint. We examined rocks and chunks of dirt to find the right color, but finally, a broken piece of ancient pottery found on site provided the

The "Moon Terrace" juts outward over a peaceful, enclosed "Sculpture Garden"—a composition of natural and human-created forms. The chimney from the guest room fireplace tapers upward into the sky.

perfect example. The paint was mixed to replicate the soft terra rosa color of the centuries-old potsherd. We painted our house in the summer of 1981, more out of necessity than following an ancient Southwest Indian tradition where the women

Handcrafted ladders replicate those seen on the roofs of old Pueblo Indian dwellings.

apply mud adobe to their Pueblo homes. Temperatures were barely tolerable at well over one hundred degrees, proof that our enthusiasm had not diminished.

Great architecture may change the way people live, but we were beginning to feel other effects as well. Three years had passed since construction began, and as the structure spiraled to its finished height, so did costs. Where did I get the impression that walls of natural boulders would reduce building costs? Johnson's vision and revision in the design process became refinement and more refinement. As with any work of art, whether a painting or sculpture in its malleable form, it is difficult to let go. That applied as well to our live-in sculpture: the artist continued to refine.

The project had taken longer than anticipated and our budget had been depleted some time previously. We were doing our best to cope with an unseemly situation: Our home in the Pacific Northwest would not sell in a depressed real estate market, and our home construction loan exceeded twenty percent. Generally speaking, things could not have been much worse, but not once did we ever speak of abandoning this site as we would later learn the ancient people before us had done, no doubt in extremely trying times. We wrestled with the one-sidedness of architectural achievement—Johnson's logo on a red tile was firmly ensconced on the entry wall; our names were firmly imprinted on our monthly mortgage payments. The design belongs to the designer forever, but at the time, it seemed that the house would belong to us for only as long as we could make the payments.

As we licked our wounds, a story appeared in *Architectural Digest* about Casa Vicens in Barcelona, one of the earliest major works of Catalan architect Antonio Gaudi (1852–1926). In it, we found a parallel to our own plight. The client, Señor Vicens, a brick merchant, was either a very adventuresome man or too concerned with selling bricks to notice the astonishing appearance of the house that later made him famous. He is said to have been all but ruined by the cost of the building, but he later became wealthy selling the brightly colored tiles that his house had popularized.

We didn't consider selling bits of boulders, but adversity is a spur to action, and we opted for a career change to creatively market residential properties. Our personal and professional emphasis on environmentally responsible architecture and site-responsive building attracted people with similar goals who wanted to live in harmony with an arid desert environment.

Living the Dream and Sharing the Vision

A striking photo by Mary E. Nichols on the February 1983 cover of *Architectural Digest* shows a ray of sunlight entering our living space through a split in the boulders. The story about Charles Johnson and the Boulder House brought natural architecture aficionados from the four directions: Architecture students arrived from Germany, and an advertising agency in Japan recognized the aura of the boulders and sent a man to find the location.

Guests walk toward the entry on a natural desert path of decomposed granite that curves past palo verde trees, saguaro cacti, and shrubs. It then meanders through a narrow passageway between boulders before the walkway transitions to terra rosa concrete and the front door comes into view. The twenty-foot-high boulder that leans imposingly over the outside pathway continues inside. After climbing the narrow stone stairway, the interior expands dramatically. Form and void combine with an ethereal presence

Sunlight enters the living space through the glazed split in the boulder wall.

Historic Zuni ollas with "Rain Bird" designs displayed on a fir beam above the library hallway. The stones on the right were the only boulders moved during construction.

that is the spirit of place to create a moving experience. The active space undeniably amplifies emotions similar to our reaction when we first encountered the outcrop of boulders. As one guest wrote, "I never would have thought a dinner invitation would turn into a spiritual experience." Johnson says that if he were granted one wish, it would be to experience the architecture as a first-time visitor.

The painter Wassily Kandinsky wrote about the power of art in his 1914 book, *The Art of Spiritual Harmony*: "The work of art is born of the artist in a mysterious and secret way. From him it gains life and being. Nor is its existence casual and inconsequent, but it has a definite and purposeful strength, alike in its material and spiritual life. It exists and has power to create spiritual atmosphere."

Our friends, Jean and Howard Lipman, renowned art collectors, looked upon the architecture as a "staggering piece of sculpture," and they brought many artists to our home: Louise Nevelson, the noted sculptor, quietly lifted her arms as if embracing the subject. Architect Philip Johnson paused to observe people moving down the stairway underneath a leaning boulder that gently touches the opposite wall. Gesturing with his hands, he repeated the movements of the people descending the stairs, and he exclaimed how beautifully the architecture frames human activities. Philip Johnson wrote us: "You are very daring. Your house still haunts me. It's by far the best use of rocks as dwelling in the world."

Charles Johnson presented the first concept sketches in January 1978, and for four years, we were emotionally involved in creating the Boulder House. We gave ourselves to a particular landscape in the experience. Johnson brought into exist-

ence a house that is perfectly at ease with the land, the climate, and us. The architecture fits in a symbolic way, in a historic way. If there is a style analogous to the house, there are echoes of the early homes in Santa Fe that are in themselves a reflection of the early Indian and Spanish influences, but not to be viewed as replicas. Our home, too, reflects features found in the region's first architecture built centuries ago, but the architecture of the Boulder House belongs here and not to any other place. It is a natural house with roots deep in the vernacular tradition, its purpose greater than we realized at that time.

In essence, architecture created the stage for the discoveries that followed.

Designed and sculpted by Cave Creek ceramists Faith Sussman and Rick Corton, the stoneware pedestal sink nestles between textured natural boulders.

Left: Window coverings created from dried saguaro ribs found on the desert and woven with rawhide strips.

Opposite page: Skylights bathe the kitchen in sunlight. Furniture designer Dale Broholm, while a student at The Evergreen State College, created the walnut stools. The boulder floor meets the stone stairway to the upper level.

An Appreciation

By Stanley Marcus

Little did Sunnie and Bill Empie realize that their decision to take advantage of huge Precambrian boulders in the Arizona desert and transform them into the walls of their home would affect their lives. This idea caused them to remold their habits and *modus operandi* and to rethink their lives.

They engaged Charles F. Johnson from Santa Fe to assume the architectural role in this innovative adventure. He proposed using the boulders as integral parts of the house that would be joined together by the use of glass panels, which would provide weatherproofing for the interior and fenestration simultaneously.

The Empies were stunned by his proposal, for they had not previously lived in an unconventional home. It looked like a simple project, but it turned into a geological monument.

They succeeded in making these immense boulders into a home that has become one of the showplaces of Arizona. The Empies are pleased that their home has an aesthetic value to others, but they feel most rewarded by the knowledge that they had recognized an historic reliquary, which they have preserved and enhanced.

Shortly after the completion of the house, I was interviewed by a publication asking my reaction to the aesthetics of the house, to which I replied, "Beauty is relative to time and space, so I can't identify any single house as the most beautiful in the world, but I have no hesitancy in saying that among the most exciting is the Boulder House in Carefree, Arizona."

Later on, in 1986, I described it for Courvoisier's *Book of the Best*. I stated that in my opinion, the most original house in America is the Empie's in Carefree, Arizona. "It's built in the midst of five gigantic boulders, connected by huge panes of glass. As you approach you think there are only boulders, but up close you are faced by the front door. Brilliant design by Charles Johnson."

Credit for this achievement must be shared by Charles Johnson and his clients, Sunnie and Bill Empie.

It took three to tango.

We had seen the stunning thirty-inch petroglyph while it was in the open and protected it while the house was under construction, at the time unaware of its significance. We pondered if the spiral form itself was meaningful to the event, and further research revealed that many cultures worldwide perceive the spiral as a two-dimensional version of the spherical vortex representing life-giving energy. The spiral order runs through nature and science, through mysticism and art. As simple as a spiral may seem, it is a complex, mystical, and universal symbol.

As we began our quest to understand the significance of the sun's interaction with the petroglyph, it was Stonehenge, the famous stone circle in Salisbury Plain, England, that first came to mind. In the 1960s, astronomer Gerald Hawkins had applied astronomy to understanding the ancient stones at Stonehenge, first constructed in 2800 B.C., and he found numerous alignments with the sun and moon. Was there more significance to the sun's interaction with the spiral? Could this site possibly be a Desert Stonehenge?

The defining moment came only months later by way of a small article in *Time* magazine, 31 January 1983, entitled "The Southwest's old Indian rock carvings were observatories." *Time* reported that the Southwest's ancient inhabitants were skilled solar observers who used rock carvings for marking calendric dates. The brief, one-column story was our first introduction to ancient astronomy in the American Southwest.

The following month, *Arizona Highways* magazine featured a story about Petrified Forest National Park in northern Arizona, which is a vast storehouse of

Preceding pages: At winter solstice sunrise, deep shadows on a weathered, south-facing boulder accentuate the faint remains of engravings—vertical grooves, meander lines, grid lines, circles with radiating lines, and a cupule in the center.

A spiral carved in stone begins with a natural curve. The symbol and the power of stone are brought together in the art—a meld of material and metaphor.

ancient scientific treasures, including rock art. Astronomer Robert A. Preston and his wife, Ann, had joined the quest to find ancient astronomical sites in the Southwest on the premise that if the indigenous people were indeed skilled sun watchers, there ought to be more examples of rock engravings that mark the changing seasons. At Petrified Forest National Park, they noticed ancient spiral and circular petroglyphs among large sandstone rocks, and they observed sunlight filtering between two large stones to form dagger-like beams that interact with the petroglyphs. They suspected that the carvings might be specific to solar observations. The Prestons have since discovered additional examples of solstice recordings at petroglyph sites in and adjacent to Petrified Forest National Park and sites in other areas of Arizona.

John B. Carlson, director of the Center for Archaeoastronomy in Maryland defines the study of ancient astronomy:

> The new discipline of archaeoastronomy seeks to learn how and what ancient peoples observed and recorded about the motions of the Sun, Moon, planets, and stars, and in what manner they integrated this astronomical knowledge into their religion, mythology, art, and daily lives.
>
> Archaeoastronomy is the interdisciplinary study of the astronomical practices, calendric systems, celestial lore, mythologies, religions, and worldviews of all ancient cultures, including the surviving indigenous peoples of today, providing new perspectives for the history of humanity's interaction with the cosmos.

Shortly after we observed the sun's interaction with the spiral petroglyph at equinox, we wrote to local colleges and universities to apprise them of this new information. At that time, we knew nothing about ancient astronomy in the Southwest, but we felt certain our discovery would be a valuable contribution to the giant puzzle of the area's prehistory. And not the courtesy of a reply. An essay several years later in *Archaeoastronomy and Ethnoastronomy News,* written by Keith Kintigh of Arizona State University, shed some light on why we had not received a reply from any of the anthropology departments. He wrote that the issue was not so much that archaeologists object to archaeoastronomy research as that they ignore it. And, the principle reason he gave was that archaeologists see archaeoastronomers as answering questions that, from a social scientific standpoint, no one is asking. He claimed his perceptions were shared by other archaeologists, which perhaps explains why our offer of information was disregarded. No one was asking.

Ray A. Williamson and other researchers in the 1970s began to observe sun-watching practices that occurred among the ancestral Puebloans in the American Southwest. Their observations and transit measurements confirmed the existence of a variety of possible solar observatories in the remains of ancient structures and at natural sites. Petroglyphs created to mark specific dates, at the time caves and rock overhangs provided shelter, were the precursor to features that the ancient people later incorporated into their architecture. At Casa Grande, for example, thirty miles south of our site, openings in the adobe walls of the building allow light to enter at certain times of the year to mark calendric dates. In addition, there are features in the remains of eleventh- and twelfth-century structures such as Pueblo Bonito at Chaco Canyon in northern New Mexico and Sun Temple at Mesa Verde that were created for the purpose of tracking the sun.

The ancient people from this cultural tradition are often referred to as Anasazi, a Navajo term that means "enemy ancestors." The term was adapted in 1936 by archaeologists to describe one of the major cultural traditions in the Southwest that also include the Hohokam, Mogollon, and Patayan. Since the term Anasazi is discomfiting to modern Pueblo people, we respectfully refer to their ancestors as the ancestral Puebloans. The modern Puebloans still live in Pueblo-like villages at the Hopi mesas in Arizona; Zuni, New Mexico; and the Western Rio Grande region of New Mexico.

Chaco Canyon was the center of attention in 1977 when participants in the

rock art field school sponsored by the Archaeological Society of New Mexico were recording rock imagery in the area. Field school participants are well-trained, certified people who scientifically map the site and graphically record its features by photographs, artists drawings, and written description. Jay Crotty, a rock art researcher, and Anna Sofaer, an artist, climbed the treacherous slope of Fajada Butte, a prominent outcrop in the canyon, to record any sites on top. They discovered spiral and concentric symbols carved in the stone. But there was more. High atop Fajada Butte, Crotty and Sofaer watched a dagger-like ray of sunlight slice through the large spiral petroglyph. Coincidently, it was at the time of the summer solstice that they observed the sun's interaction with the petroglyph. Further observations have revealed that the two spirals mark both equinox and solstice. The scientific community received the new information about Fajada Butte with some trepidation as the "Sun Dagger" solstice marker was publicized and analyzed. The discovery brought ancient astronomy to the general public's attention, and people began to make pilgrimages to the site. Now, the stones on Fajada Butte are off limits to the public as the well-trodden path was altering the positions of the stones.

The delicate pink flowers of
a fairy duster, *Calliandra
eriophylla.*

Mexican Gold Poppies, *Eschscholtzia mexicana*, bloom profusely in the spring.

Tall, thorny branches of the ocotillo, *Fouquieria splendens*, spring to life after a rain with tiny leaves and brilliant red blossoms that last only as long as the plant retains moisture. In the foreground, the creamy white blossoms of the yucca plant, *Yucca*.

Summer Solstice

Gentle earth tremors would not accompany every forthcoming revelation at the Boulder House, but such was the heralding of a second major discovery—that of the four-pointed petroglyph. At the end of a long day spent painting our house, Bill was cleaning paint brushes, and I was resting on the terrace when he walked toward me, looking shocked. "Did you feel that?" he asked. "Feel what?" I questioned. Bill explained that the earth had shuddered, and I never doubted for a moment that was exactly what he meant. I pondered his statement while staring into space toward the boulder straight ahead. Then, the petroglyph carved on the vertical face of the boulder came into focus much in the same way that a 35 mm transparency image "pops" into focus on the screen. Forty feet directly in front of me, a petroglyph assumed its visible form—a symbol approximately six feet high, with four triangular points extending outward from the circle in the center. The stone carving was unmistakable as sunlight glanced across the boulder at an oblique angle. Shadows fell into the deep grooves and emphasized its form.

How could we possibly have overlooked a petroglyph so large and so distinct? Even more astonishing, it appears in photos taken of the site before construction of our home, yet we were unaware of its presence. It was somewhat reassuring to find an explanation for our oversight when we read that archaeological records include cases of prehistoric art overlooked because the persons did not expect to see anything. Our eyes generally see a blend of the place at which we are looking, so discoveries often depend on our expectations and current state of mind. The stunning art in one of Spain's most famous caves, Altamira, was initially overlooked. Later, a child saw the images of bison painted on the ceiling in the cavern when her father returned to excavate the cave.

Again, the *Time* magazine article came to mind. The story convincingly supported ancient astronomical practices in the Southwest, but it was the photograph of Preston, with his cheek pressed against a spiral carved in stone, that gave me pause and altered my perception of the petroglyphs. He was sighting across a petroglyph on the rock's face toward the distant horizon. For no particular reason, I presumed that petroglyphs were to be viewed frontally. Clearly, I needed to look at them from another perspective. I returned to the four-pointed symbol, pressed my cheek against the cold stone, and looked northeastward toward the horizon. From

my observation, the petroglyph appeared to be aligned to where the sun would rise at summer solstice, which allowed that the carving might be another calendrical marker. However, there was not an obvious place where a shaft of sunlight could originate and interact with the petroglyph.

It was a long wait to June 21, the longest day of the year, to see if the symbol would mark the summer solstice. We arose before dawn to salute the sunrise. The sun's first light rose above the horizon and cast an elongated shadow of the boulder outcrop across the desert morning, and then the shadow quietly and slowly receded back into itself. With freshly brewed coffee in hand, we sat on the terrace and focused on the petroglyph in anticipation that something might occur.

The soft morning light gently washed the sunrise side of the boulder, and there was still no clue how the sun would reach the south-facing side of the boulder where the petroglyph was located. We continued to stare at the circle carved in

A magnificent six-foot-high petroglyph awaits the sun's arrival at summer solstice. Sunlight washes the sunrise side of the boulder as a small sundagger appears within the center of the petroglyph.

The sundagger lengthens until it fully penetrates the center of the circle to signal the longest day of the year and the sun's completion of its northward journey. Sequential imagery on the following pages.

stone. Then at 6:15 a.m., a brilliant small circle of sunlight, no bigger than a dime, appeared in the center of the circle. We were stunned. The sunrise side of the massive boulder had been sculpted so that a pencil-thin line of sunlight could break through and meet the petroglyph. The circle expanded into a small triangular pointer, and then the pointer slowly elongated until it fully penetrated the concave depression in the center of the petroglyph at 6:27 a.m. It was awesome. I wanted to call "stop!" After long moments of anticipation, that is what it did. The light lay motionless in the groove—the sun and the symbol in a long, sensuous embrace. Forty-five minutes later, the sun began to stir, and the sunlight flowed slowly outward from the concave groove in the center of the circle.

The magic of that first hour is not lost, as each year at summer solstice we watch the visually stunning occurrence created by ancient hands. The magnificent six-foot-high symbol carved in stone celebrates the completion of the sun's north-

ward journey. We feel a connection across space and time with the people who watched the same event so many centuries ago. It is a profoundly moving experience. First the exciting incident at equinox, and now the solar interaction with another petroglyph at summer solstice. Both confirmed that, indeed, this truly is a special place—a place where the sacred was made visible.

Rock imagery is the single most visible manifestation of a prehistoric belief system, and the site's features also give us insight into the role astronomy played. Perhaps as high as ten percent of rock art sites in the American Southwest have an association with a solstice or an equinox. The enduring markings in stone affirm the importance the ancient people gave to honoring and reinforcing cosmic order. Certainly, this would not surprise contemporary Hopi, Zuni, and native people of the Rio Grande villages who recognize the interlinking of the sun with rock calendars as part of the sacred nature of such sites. Calendrical ceremonialism distinguishes Puebloan beliefs most clearly from those of other traditional cultures in Western North America. Continuing to honor their responsibilities to keep natural forces and all living things in harmony and balance, the Southwest's native people still monitor solar and lunar cycles to determine the time for celebrations and ritual that are important to their worldview. Rina Swentzell, Santa Clara Pueblo, explains Pueblo sacred space:

The foothill palo verde tree, *Cercidium microphyllum*, blooms in May—a brilliant display of gold.

Visually and physically understating shrines, or for that matter, Pueblo community and house forms, stems from the very nature of Pueblo cosmology. At the center of the Pueblo belief system is the conviction that people are not separate from nature and natural forces. This insoluble connection with nature has existed from the beginning of time. The goal of human existence is to maintain wholeness or oneness with the natural universe.

THE EMPIE PETROGLYPH SITE AZ U: 1: 165 (ASM)

WAS PLACED ON THE

NATIONAL REGISTER OF HISTORIC PLACES

AUGUST 31,1998

THE NATIONAL REGISTER OF HISTORIC PLACES IS THE FEDERAL GOVERNMENT'S OFFICIAL
AND PRESTIGIOUS LIST OF PROPERTIES WORTHY OF PRESERVATION.

THE SITE'S EXTRAORDINARY FEATURES INCLUDE BAS-RELIEF VULVA-FORM PETROGLYPHS CARVED IN GRANITIC STONE.
THE ANCIENT PEOPLE OF THE AMERICAN SOUTHWEST WERE SKILLED SOLAR OBSERVERS AND HERE, MAJOR CALENDRIC EVENTS
WINTER AND SUMMER SOLTICE, AUTUMN AND SPRING EQUINOX ARE MARKED BY SOLAR INTERACTION WITH CIRLE AND SPIRAL PETROGLYPHS.

SUMMER SOLTICE SEQUENTIAL IMAGERY BY HART W. EMPIE

Winter solstice sunrise

Winter Solstice

Just before winter solstice 1996, Bill made yet another astonishing discovery on his daily sunrise walk with our dog, Bertou, a Bouvier des Flandres. Bill returned and said, "Come outside. You are not going to believe this." We pondered the significance of innumerable subtle markings we had noticed on a twenty-foot-high boulder, but not until that winter solstice morning did the carvings become clearly visible.

Bill had paused at a distance to look at the glow on the southwest-facing boulder as the rising sun glanced across its broad surface at an oblique angle. Faint outlines of circles carved in the stone came into focus, some with radiating lines. Sweeping grooves across the vast boulder embraced some of the circles. It was mind-boggling to witness this spectacular discovery. The rhythm of lines and circles created by an ancient artist was dazzling, if not the discovery itself. Temperature and weather had worn the boulder away over the centuries, but the rock carvings are still visible to the discerning eye when the light is just right.

What finally brought the obscure engravings into view was the distance from which Bill viewed the boulders and also the shadows in the grooves created by the angle of the rising sun at winter solstice. By noon, the faint images of the carvings receded into the boulder. Indeed, it was a morning to celebrate with cold champagne and warm coffeecake. Each new day, we made ourselves comfortable at a distance from the boulder with steaming, strong coffee in our hands. With Bill's

An occasional snowfall can occur at an elevation of 2,300 feet in the high Sonoran Desert.

Leica camera and tripod firmly in place, we watched our morning light show on an ancient artist's stone canvas. The importance of light and shadow cannot be overstated, particularly lighting at an oblique angle that deepens shadow and emphasizes form. Rock art researchers understand this as they sometimes return to a place where they earlier observed petroglyphs and they are difficult to find. How well the ancient artisan understood these subtle nuances when creating the messages in stone; messages that can keep their silence in the brightest light of day.

The symbols on the south-facing boulder include the same abstract patterns found in the earliest rock engravings throughout the world—parallel lines, meanders, zigzags, spirals, circles, dots, nested curves, and grid lines or netting. Recognizing the commonality of these images, scientists are exploring the possibility that they relate to shamanism, the oldest of belief systems among humankind. Cultures worldwide relied on persons with extraordinary power, male and female, who were healers or intermediaries with the spirit world to benefit the community. Shamans had vision quests and experienced traveling to other dimensions while in an altered state of consciousness. Researchers are looking at rock imagery from the perspective that it was painted or carved by shamans to record their trance experiences.

David Lewis-Williams, a South African scholar of cave art who had access to descendants of the South African San Bushmen, set off the idea of the relationship of rock art to shamanism. Lewis-Williams, along with South African Thomas Dowson, studied the rock paintings and carvings of the San and developed a neuropsychological model of the mental imagery of trance states. Further ethnographic accounts and neuropsychological studies now suggest that as shamans enter the first stage of a trance state, they experience phosphenes, within-the-eye visual phenomena that include zigzags, dots, grids, vortexes, parallel or meandering lines. A shaman painted or engraved in stone the images seen in his altered state of consciousness. This became a record of the mystic trance experience, a reminder of the journey, and ensured the shaman's continued power.

Jessica Jarvis's spontaneous and unspoiled art at age three reveals the same entoptic patterns that an ancient artist recreated on a stone canvas—spirals, sun, radiating lines, circles with dots, concentric circles, sunbursts, meander lines, and vertical lines.

The concept has tweaked the interest of archaeologists in the United States. David S. Whitley, for instance, writes that far western North American ethnography universally and unequivocally supports a connection between rock art, altered states of consciousness, and shamanic beliefs and practices. While discussions about the relationship of rock art to shamanism broadened among rock art researchers in this country, Jean Clottes, advisor on prehistoric art to the French ministry of culture, wrote that the great art of Europe's Paleolithic caves can be best understood through the lens of shamanism.

Fourteen years had passed since we first witnessed solar interaction with a spiral petroglyph at equinox and solar interaction within a circle to mark the summer solstice. Notably absent was the place that would honor winter solstice, which occurs around December 22 when the sun has reached its southernmost

position in the sky. Winter is the time when the sun's power is at its weakest and is interpreted as dying. Earth sleeps, animals and snakes hibernate, and plants become dormant. Historically, Native Americans in the Southwest have carried on ceremonies during the winter solstice season to encourage the return of the sun's life-giving light and energy and to celebrate the rebirth of the sun as it resumes its journey northward while the days begin to lengthen. Among Puebloans, it is a time of reverence and respect for the spirit beings and also a time for storytelling. Considering its continued importance among many tribes in the American Southwest, we felt certain that the early people at this site recorded the winter solstice, as they did other

Right: At winter solstice, a dagger of sunlight moves slowly into the rear of the space to enter a small hole carved near the topside.

Left: A space carved in the boulder may have been a place for offerings to celebrate the return of the light at winter solstice.

cyclical dates—but where?

Finally, the elusive solstice marker was revealed the same winter that Bill first noticed the engravings on the southwest boulder. The Empie Petroglyph Site was under review for nomination to the National Register of Historic Places. Bruce Masse, one of several professional archaeologists who reviewed the site's features, suggested that we pay particular attention to an ovoid cavity near the base of a large boulder. The large enhanced space, about eighteen inches high and two feet in depth and width, appeared as an ancient stone altar. In fact, we had been referring to it as a stone altar. Masse believed the positions of the adjacent boulders opposite the cavity would create a dagger of sunlight that might enter the space at winter solstice. If that occurred, he said it might have been a place for offerings. The Southwest's Puebloan societies are known to have places called Sun Shrines that have a focused sacred significance where prayer sticks and offerings were made to encourage the sun's return.

Two weeks before winter solstice, we began to observe the altar at mid-afternoon. Solar interaction with petroglyphs may occur as early as three weeks before solstices, although the time period for this prelude varies among ancient solar observatories in the Southwest. The light interaction at Holly

House at Hovenweep National Monument, for example, occurs at sunrise for twenty days on either side of solstice. There may be esoteric reasons for the sunwatcher to have announced ceremonies well ahead of the actual date, and practically speaking, the anticipatory date most likely allowed time to prepare for the requisite feast and/or ritual.

A dagger of sunlight appeared from between the two adjacent boulders and moved slowly across the desert floor. Each day, it moved only slightly toward the altar space. The winter solstice date arrived, and despite my verbal coaching, the dagger of sunlight was not going to enter the space. The sun's position in the southern sky was close to standstill, hence the name solstice. In other words, during the four days before and after the date of the solstice, it is not possible for the eye to detect any change in the position of the sun. That allowed additional

days for me to pursue this notion. The next afternoon, I returned each hour to observe the space itself to see what might occur. Finally, a sundagger appeared on the boulder *above* the altar and slowly worked its way downward into the space. The point of the sundagger then curved under the upper edge of the altar and narrowed into a thin point as it entered the human-made space at 3:30 p.m. Its source had not been obvious. As with the summer solstice marker, the boulder that held the altar had been enhanced to allow the light to enter.

Remarkably, there was more. I hunkered down in order to watch the pointer as it narrowed and crept deep into the rear of the cavity, finally to enter a small hole carved near the ceiling. There it rested for a moment, and then the light disappeared. The sundagger can only penetrate the small hole when the sun is at its lowest southernmost position. The interaction clearly emphasizes the sun's importance to all life on earth, and honors its rebirth at winter solstice. Looking across a vast expanse of desert in the quiet moments before the winter sun set far to the southwest, I sensed how important it must have been for the people to follow ritual and ceremony to help turn the sun around. Darkness descends across the desert in late afternoon. It is an ominous time before the sun begins its journey northward and daylight lengthens.

The next morning in the crispness of a high desert dawn, Bill and I walked around the boulders that embrace our home, and in front of a cave, we were greeted by a large potsherd lying in plain view on the barren path. I had asked for guidance to locate the winter solstice marker, and it appeared that our resident spirit guides were again reminding us of their presence.

The site's astronomical features shed another light on two shaped ceramic discs which have a hole drilled from each side, creating an hourglass perforation in the center. Similar discs, skewered on a wooden rod to create a sunstick, have been noted as ceremonial apparatus at ancient astronomy sites around the world. At Bowers Cave in Southern California, for example, a stone disk on top of a wooden shaft symbolized the sun with painted rays. The Chumash Sun Priest would insert the sunstick into the earth during solstice ceremonies so that the earth would be energized by the sun.

Solar interaction or alignment with petroglyphs was one manner in which important calendrical events were anticipated and marked during the time people occupied caves and rock shelters; the other, the horizon calendar. Historically among the Puebloan people, the sun's movement was tracked by a sunwatcher who noted distinctive points along the horizon where the sun rises or sets to calculate more accurately the date for ceremonies. Presumably, the sharp peaks and clefts of

the distant mountains would have been as familiar to a sunwatcher as the ridges on the back of his/her hand. From our outcrop of boulders, it is possible to see the horizon as a complete circle under the dome of the sky.

Some contemporary Native American tribes still honor the importance of the horizon calendar, and it is not uncommon to have a place in the home where sunlight enters and touches to mark the time of year. When Charles Loloma, Hopi artist and Sun Priest, visited us, he sat facing a window and looked to the east over the vast desert landscape to the distant mountains beyond. "This would be a good place for a horizon calendar," he mused.

My poem, painted on our bedroom wall in calligraphy by artist Philip Grainger, is in essence our horizon calendar at the Boulder House. The gray light of dawn appears and outlines the poem. The yellow light of dawn brings the words into focus, and as the sun breaks over the distant mountains, the graceful lettering enhanced with gold shadow outlining is revealed anew in the bright morning sunlight. Simply beautiful. In the language of northern Inuit people, the words "to make poetry" and "to breathe" are from the same root, the word for soul.

◎

Awake, sweet Earth to the
warmth of the Sun's first Rays
and the glow of Renewal.

Rock Imagery and Revelations
The Feminine Generative Principle

North American Indians paid tribute to a wide variety of spiritual forces, but few were more important or more powerful than the spirit in stone. The enduring power in stone was so well known that it was singled out and named in many native groups. Among the Lakota, for example, the stone was known as Inyan, the first substance. With all the power they contained, rocks were frequently chosen as places for worship. The power in the rocks is evident at the Empie site. The intent of the makers of the petroglyphs is clear—they wanted to be associated with the power.

—Lawrence Loendorf, Research Professor

Department of Sociology and Anthropology, New Mexico State University

Some people see stones as silent sentinels. Some say wistfully, "If only the rocks could talk." A millennium ago, tapping sounds echoed among the cluster of boulders as an artisan wielded a hammerstone and created symbols in the granite to honor the life-giving force of Nature. The petroglyphs remain where the ancient artist carved them in stone, but they are not silent. Just as words are formed to express ideas and feelings, the words in and of themselves are simply symbols that have no intrinsic meaning until the receiver of the message decodes them into thoughts or images. Likewise, the symbols that transmit the worldview of an ancient culture require decoding into the thoughts that are the source, the wellspring, of those symbols. It is not by accident that what the visionary has seen appears on stone. Stone endures. The people who created these symbols intended that their message should last for generations, much as we might employ a time capsule to inform future inhabitants of the earth about our culture.

More than twenty vulvaform petroglyphs have been found among the boulders that embrace our home. Ancient pictographs and petroglyphs that represent the female genitalia are most often abstract forms, such as a simple bisected circle or oval. However, largely due to the propensity of the granitic stone, they appear as bas-relief sculptural forms. Not to be overlooked is the large vulvaform that became permanent wall art in our dining room. The petroglyph is eight feet high, four feet wide, and ten inches deep.

The imposing, eight-foot-high vulvaform adjacent to an old *trastero* (New Mexican cupboard) draped with an antique Navajo weaving.

Ancient vulvaform petroglyph flanked by jojoba shrub, *Simmondsia chinensis.*

The form was sculpted around a natural fissure by pecking away bits of granite with a lithic tool. Ken Hedges, curator at the San Diego Museum of Man, leaned against a low wall in the dining room. Pointing to the large vulvaform on the natural boulder wall, he asked if we knew what we had there. Indeed, we were aware of several similar forms in the boulders that appeared to be representations of the female genitalia, which in fact prompted occasional jesting.

Hedges' research at sites in Southern California had revealed similar petroglyphs, but he remarked that this was the first vulva symbol carved in granite that he had seen outside the California sites. He sent us a copy of Charlotte McGowan's paper, *Ceremonial Fertility Sites in California,* that had just been published in 1982. We were startled to see photos of sculptural vulvaforms similar to

those at our site. She chose to use the ancient Sanskrit word, yoni, a word for the female organ of generation, for the natural (or occasionally enhanced) features, as opposed to carved or painted representations of the vulva in rock art. McGowan had consulted with the local Indians, and they affirmed that the stones resembling the female form had been used for fertility-enhancing rituals. Learning that sites not 200 miles from our location have natural and enhanced vulvaforms was not only a revelation, but also an inspiration to find out more about this ancient symbol. While fertility seemed a likely explanation, we sensed the vulva symbols at our site held greater meaning.

The strong definition of the ancient vulvaform in our dining room and its numinous presence bring to mind a passage from Zuni mythology. In their migration story, they named places followed by the repetitive phrase, "here we get up and move on." For example, "We come to stone-lodged-in-a-cleft place; here we get up and move on. We come to stone-picture place; here we get up and move on." The myth's poetic description spurs the question of cultural connections, as many tribes passed this way during their migrations millennia ago. Mathilde Stevenson lived among the Zunis and recorded the culture's practices in 1904,

Left: An eighteen-inch vulvaform petroglyph at twelve feet above ground level.

The female genitalia represented simply as a circle with a slash through the center. A triangle appears to the left within the roughly executed carving.

saying the place called Mother Rock was a shrine visited by couples to pray and leave offerings before the birth of a child. The rising sun at winter solstice strikes a point at the southwest end of Corn Mountain at Zuni where the vulvaform petroglyphs are dominant. The power possibly inherent to our site has not been verified, but visitors who are hoping to have a child do not overlook the opportunity to enhance their chances for pregnancy or successful birthing by placing their hands on the stone to receive any benefits that might be forthcoming.

We looked to Native American views for an understanding of the imagery at our site as well as to discussions of the universal similarity of rock art. The female vulva as a metaphoric symbol, we discovered, is found in the earliest traditional cultures worldwide where Nature was revered and the female was glorified as the Creatrix, generator of the species and Goddess of regeneration. Humankind shared the capacity of using metaphor as a way to express that which could not be fully understood.

The defining moment in our quest to understand the imagery at our site was the 1989 publication, *The Language of the Goddess: Unearthing the Hidden Symbols of Western Civilization*. The extensive research of ancient iconography by Marija Gimbutas, Professor Emeritus of Archaeology at University of California at Los Angeles, profoundly changed the way people view ancient symbols. Gimbutas evaluated thousands of symbolic artifacts and imagery from the earliest Neolithic (7000-3500 B.C.) village sites of Europe to establish that matricentric societies honored the feminine generative principle. She writes, "Symbols are seldom abstract in any genuine sense; their ties with Nature persist, to be discovered through the study of context and association. The main theme of the ancient symbolism is the mystery of birth and death and the renewal of life, not only human, but all life on Earth and indeed in the whole cosmos."

The universal similarity of symbols that persist through time and across space was addressed by Swiss psychologist Carl Jung (1875-1961). Jung theorizes that the symbols occurring in cultures worldwide at various times come from a genetically inherited structure that he calls the "collective unconscious," containing memories of our primordial past that remain within each of us. Jung notes that many of these societies were independent of each other, yet the same impulses arose spontaneously wherever there were people.

The native cultures of the American Southwest are amazingly diverse, but the commonality of their beliefs centers on a relationship with Mother Earth and with

The eight-foot-high vulvaform was sculpted or enhanced to a depth of ten inches.

all living things. According to Native American scholar Paula Gunn Allen, "Tribal systems have been operating in the 'new world' for several hundred thousand years. It is unlikely that a few hundred years of colonization will see their undoing. For millennia, American Indians have based their social systems, however diverse, on ritual, spirit-centered, woman-focused world-views."

Following a vertical fissure in the stone at the top of a twenty-foot-high boulder are three connecting vulvaforms, each over two feet long.

Allen's informative writing offered for us further insight into the meaning of the symbols found at this site along with its greater purpose. She writes from a Pueblo Indian woman's perspective and addresses the universal life force and beliefs of her ancestors in her book *Sacred Hoop: Recovering the Feminine in American Indian Traditions.*

"In the beginning was thought, and her name was Woman. The Mother, the Grandmother, recognized from earliest times into the present, celebrated in social structures, architecture, and the oral tradition. . . To assign to this great being the position of fertility goddess is exceedingly demeaning: it trivializes the tribes and it trivializes the power of woman." Allen cites a Keres Indian ceremonial prayer, a literal translation by Anthony Purley, a Laguna writer, as a most illuminating expression of a traditional cultural belief: " 'She is mother of us all, after Her, mother earth follows, in fertility, in holding, and taking again us back to her breast.' "

Left: The gentle curves and features of the massive boulder are analogous to the feminine body. The prominent labial form (above) appears in the center of the fissure, and at 15 feet above ground level, a relatively small vulvaform assumes an imposing presence.

Right: The serpentine carving reaches from the earth to connect with the prominent vulvaform petroglyph.

Some archaeologists decry that Euro-Americans could have any understanding of the ancient practices of the native people in this land. However, the animistic worldview of the pre-Christian Europeans would suggest otherwise. Our DNA represents our individual hereditary characteristics, the heritage of millennia past, and our soul connection to the past. Bill Moyers, television commentator, eloquently said in a taped interview with mythologist Joseph Campbell, "What most do not know, is that the remnants of all that 'stuff' line the walls of our interior system of belief, like shards of broken pottery in an archaeological site."

The roots of the Western psyche are connected to a worldview and ancient practices with strong shamanistic elements. The Poetic Edda, written down in the thirteenth century in Iceland, contains pre-Christian Germanic-Nordic myths and legends, ancestral stories of the ancient gods and goddesses, as told by the elder mothers. Edda means "great-grandmother" in the Old Norse language.

In pre-Christian Europe, it was the vision of the völva that offered understanding of cosmogonic origins and of the age-old cycles of cosmic death and renewal. The cosmos was structured like other shamanistic cosmologies, as a threefold or ninefold world, arranged along a central world tree. Travel between realms was the role of a female shaman, völva, while in an altered state of consciousness. Freyja, goddess of the seeresses, and the völvas were famed for their ability to look back to the origins of the world. While the name völva was startling in its familiarity, it means "staff carrier," based on an Old Norse word, völ.

Various configurations of the vulva symbol are found throughout our site, such as three connecting vulvaforms about six feet long that follow a vertical crack in the stone. Another set of three, carved side by side, follow along a natural horizontal fissure. The remarkable integration of a vulvaform connected to a serpentine carving appears as if the snake emerges from Mother Earth and reaches upward to connect with the petroglyph. In human life, the umbilical cord is itself a serpentine connection between the mother and new life. The position of the cord at the posterior fold of the vulva implies birthing, or perhaps signifies a birthing place.

Left: A weathered face appears in the center of the boulder.

Often, there is more than meets the eye when first viewing ancient imagery carved in stone. The large, fifteen-foot-high vulvaform on a west-facing boulder is an example of how the space must be viewed holistically within the context of its setting. Further, we should examine the consonance, or harmony, of the parts that make up the whole and the shape of the space that contains them—and us. In this case, the form encompasses much of the massive boulder, its gentle curves and features analogous to the feminine body. Our eyes focus at first on the prominent labial form in the center of the crack in the vast boulder, then to the surprising discovery of a relatively small vulvaform about two feet long that was sculpted at the top of the fissure.

Right: A V-shape form sits prominently on the boulder in front of the petroglyph that marks the summer solstice. The abstract form also is seen as handles or decoration on ancient Southwest and Mesoamerican pottery.

The sizes of the petroglyphs range upward from eighteen inches, although most are about thirty inches long. Perhaps the larger sizes are not so much a stylistic decision as a practical one considering the coarseness of the stone's granitic surface. The small glyphs seen in this region, generally attributed to the Hohokam people, were executed on a smooth surface stone such as basalt. They are shallow and distinct because of the contrast in color from pecking through the dark patinated veneer known as desert varnish, exposing the fresh rock surface beneath.

Right: A vulvaform was created around a small fissure in the boulder in the center of the photo

While the rock imagery is not framed in the Western sense, it was executed within spaces defined by fissures in the stone or the curvature of the boulders. Often, the fissures and natural declivities in the rock face were incorporated into the symbol. By incorporating a natural feature of the stone, the power associated with stone could enter and empower the symbol, thereby strengthening its life force. The symbol and the spiritual power of stone are brought together in the art—a meld of material and metaphor. It appears that the artisan made choices because in places

141

where there are cracks and natural stone declivities that suggest placement of a vulvaform, no vulva symbols exist.

A new concept in the interpretation of rock imagery suggests that certain locations may have been selected because of the resonance of the stone or perhaps the acoustics of the space. Sculptors understand the power and resonance of stone. Apache sculptor Allan Houser said, "Stone lives, just as surely as we do." Noguchi, the distinguished sculptor who spent his life working with stone, stated, "When I tap it, I get the echo of that which we are."

Other symbolic petroglyphs that would support a theme of regeneration at this site are the snake, bear paw, and butterfly petroglyphs: The snake not only replicates the power of spiral energy as it coils and then springs outward, but also is a symbol of regeneration, since it sheds its old skin when new skin appears. The snake and the bear symbolize renewal as they awaken from winter hibernation. The butterfly is a symbol of regeneration and the embodiment of transformation based upon its dramatic change from one life form into another.

There are few recorded sites across the North American continent that have an abundance of bas-relief vulva petroglyphs such as those in the Yubey area of Baja California, Mexico; Southern California; eastward to the prominent site at Mother Rock at Zuni's Corn Mountain, New Mexico; and at Peterborough, Ontario, Canada. The large concentration of

Natural sacred places include springs, caves, and rock formations that have the potential to move the human mind into those spaces.

twenty vulvaforms at our site is the first reported in Arizona. Since the symbol itself is not commonly found at rock art sites, perhaps the few places where concentrations of vulva symbols occur represent women's spaces associated with life cycle rituals, a gathering place for women, or a birthing place. They may also have been places of pilgrimage. Archaeologist David S. Whitley noted that shamans were willing to trek great distances to sacred places imbued with a power specific to healing, fertility, dreaming or vision questing. Moreover, shamans oftentimes traveled from a different cultural or ethnolinguistic territory to a place of power.

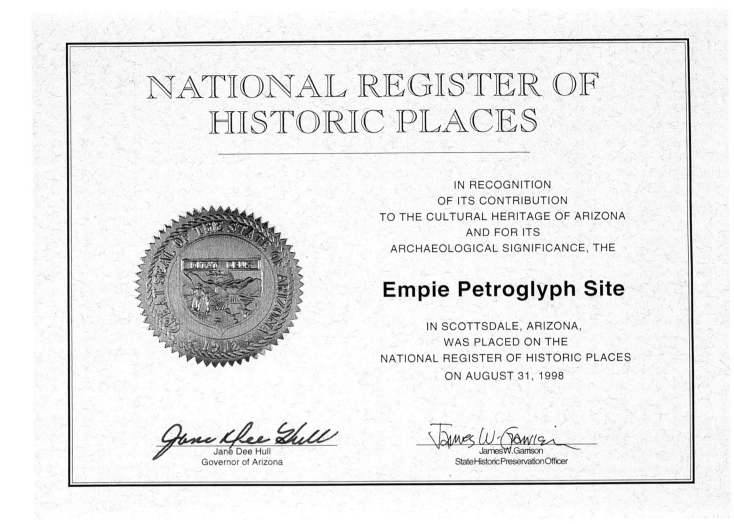

Twenty years after we had seen the first petroglyph, and after years of research, site number AZ U: 1: 165 (ASM) was assigned by the Arizona State Museum, one of two places in Arizona that registers archaeological sites. We began the arduous process through the State Historic Preservation Office to list the site on the National Register of Historic Places. Archaeologists Todd Bostwick, Bruce Masse, Lawrence Loendorf, currently president of the American Rock Art Research Association, and Chris Loendorf reviewed the site's features and supported the nomination of The Empie Petroglyph Site AZ U: 1: 165 (ASM) to the National Register of Historic Places, August 1998.

We have scanned other granite boulders in the surrounding area for petroglyphs, and we have found only a few solitary vulvaforms located at uncommonly beautiful places where one can look out over the vast desert. The scattered locations give credence to the concept that the symbol held profound meaning to the ancient people, and they carved in stone the feminine symbol of generation to honor the beauty and fecundity of the earth. We stand in the same place where people centuries ago stood, and we too honor the beauty that remains. On the other hand, perhaps the symbols were offered as a prayer at a time when the land and the resources were in peril from alternating floods and drought centuries ago, and we can understand that, too.

In writing about the symbols carved on stone, I have attempted in most instances to use the words "rock imagery" because some Native Americans dislike the term "rock art." Art is such an integral part of their lifeway that there is no word in their language that sets it apart. The contemporary Puebloan artists, however, accept art and artists as words of positive distinction associated with the success and recognition of their creative work. Art is distinctively human, such as our power of language. Indeed, art *is* a language—a form of communication. If it were not for that deeply embedded language within humankind, we would not be the recipients of these ancient messages.

Years have passed since we saw the first of many petroglyphs at this site. I stood quietly one evening at dusk under a leaning boulder to shelter myself from a soft female rain. In the waning light, the outline of a petroglyph on the vertical face of the boulder in front of me slowly assumed its shape as the gentle rain moistened the dark patina around the carving. I contemplated the appearance of a mountain sheep carved in the stone, and I asked aloud, "Why did you wait so long to introduce yourself?"

My eyes glanced across vast granite boulder walls, and I wondered what might be revealed next.

@

Atop a balanced boulder, a
circle petroglyph is carved in
the stone.

Caves as Shelters
Caves as Sacred Places

Previous page: Sunlight enters the cave through the sky opening. The contemporary handcrafted ladder replicates the symbolic ladder seen in a Pueblo ceremonial room.

Bending low to avoid the spider's web that guards the portal, and entering the cool cavern carved within the stone, was like stepping into another time and place. The air hung heavy with the imprint of centuries past. And above me, the ceiling was encrusted with the carbon of ancient fires. Through the opening of the ceiling, an anthropomorphic figure carved in the boulder high overhead appeared as a guardian spirit, its watchful eyes looking down into the chamber. I sat quietly, embraced by the coolness of the cave on a hot desert day. Minuscule particles of dust danced in the narrow ray of sunlight penetrating the dusky cave, as I pondered its significance.

The cave is located at the base of the exterior side of the west "wall" of the boulder outcrop. The land slopes downward from the opening, creating the feeling of a lofty position overlooking the desert landscape and beyond to the dark, gray-blue mountains. The interior space is shaped like the letter D. One side of the room is concave, while the natural stone of the opposite side slants slightly inward. The irregular-shaped space is approximately six feet wide and eight feet deep, with a ceiling height of six feet.

Caves and rock shelters were natural habitats for Stone Age hunters and gatherers, and for millennia, the ancient sanctuaries also have been part of humankind's experience and spiritual vision. At our site, the ancient carbon stain on the underside of a vast boulder reclining on another rock indicates that the space had been used. Soft lighting entered through a fissure in the stone to silhouette a pottery jar (olla) in a narrow niche. Beside the olla, two carbon-encrusted bowls and a shallow, elongated scoop were inverted, as if someone had washed the dishes and turned them over to dry.

Just outside the cave, sixteen inches below the present ground level, we also discovered an oval slab of stone (metate) used for grinding. Underneath the worn, overturned metate was a round, hand-held grinding stone (mano). They had been placed there centuries ago. Did someone plan to use the tools again, or was the metate simply too heavy to carry? Perhaps they were left behind for the next people who would pass this way.

Left: The beautifully sculpted portal to the cave reflects the feminine theme. At upper left, a three-dimensional anthropomorphic figure appears as a guardian of the site.

The stone cavern, however, exudes a presence that transcends the idea of a rock shelter as habitat. The triangular-shaped entrance to the cave emphasizes the importance of the threshold through which life emerges. Caves, crevices, and caverns of the earth have long been considered natural manifestations of the primordial womb of the mother as far back as Paleolithic time, when narrow passages, oval-shaped areas, and caves were marked in red. Since that time, the vulva, the vestibule of the vagina through which life emerges, is sometimes represented as a triangle. The pubic triangle is not an expression of physiology, but rather a symbol of the vulva and the cosmic womb of the Earth Mother.

At equinox, the cave is filled with late afternoon sunlight. When we earlier witnessed the sun reaching the hole created within the altar space at winter solstice, that occasion suggested we likewise observe several small holes along a fissure in the stone cave at winter solstice. It became apparent that the mouth of the cave was enhanced, or carved, so that just before the sun recedes behind the distant mountains, the dim shaft of sunlight can extend deep into the rear of the cave and enter the holes along a diagonal crack in the rear wall. Perhaps they, too, were created to receive the sun's life-giving energy. It followed, also, that the row of

Right: The fading light at winter solstice sunset brushes against the dusky wall at the rear of the cave, follows a fissure in the stone, and enters several holes. In the foreground, a grinding stone (metate) and handstone (mano.)

cupules on the opposite side of the cave floor interacts with a shaft of light entering the cave at summer solstice.

When the sun penetrates a symbol or enters the cave, it is remarkable that a hole or entry has been created to receive the sun, a feature that appears to honor the procreative power of the sun. The sun enters the space, the womb of the earth, as well as the vulvaform to symbolize birth and regeneration.

The carbon stain on the ceiling prompted me to look for signs of a firepit. I scraped aside about two inches of dirt and rock fragments that covered the cave's stone floor and was startled to find a passageway that angles downward through the stone about four feet before it turns. Its distance and purpose are left consigned to the imagination. A tunnel approximately sixteen inches in diameter might not be considered large enough for human access, but there are other examples of passages that narrow almost to impassability. Over five yards of the passageway to Arrow Grotto at Feather Cave in south central New Mexico, for instance, is only twelve inches high and twenty-four inches wide. Investigators moved through the crawlway by lying flat with arms stretched out, pushing with their toes and pulling with their fingers. The Meander passage at the Paleolithic Lascaux Cave in France narrows to sixteen inches, yet figures are painted within the space.

Before we became aware of the significance of our site, the west-facing cave was just a lovely, calm place to be, far removed from the din of homebuilding in progress. Then, as we learned about the early people in the American Southwest, the cave assumed other dimensions. Myths differ slightly among the Southwest's tribes, but creation stories explain how their worlds came into existence. In their stories, the place from which the first people emerged into the present world may take the form of a cave, spring, or passageway.

Inside the cave, the ceiling is encrusted with carbon from fires. A sixteen-inch diameter passageway (left foreground) descends into the stone floor of the cave.

In Hopi myth, Spider Grandmother reminds the people that they came from the Lower World for a purpose: "When you build your kivas, place a small Sípàapuni (symbolic emergence place) there in the floor to remind you where you come from and what you are looking for. Those who forget why they came to this world will lose their way. They will disappear in the wilderness and be forgotten." She also told the people to leave their marks on the rocks and cliffs wherever they stop and rest—so that others will know who was there before.

Within the remains of the kivas constructed by the ancestral Pueblo people, one can still see the symbolic openings that were replicated in the floors. Rina Swentzell, observes that:

> The kiva structure was totally symbolic. Its rooftop was like the pueblo plaza space from where we could connect with the sky, while the rooftop opening took us into the kiva structure which was like going back into the earth via the *nansipu* [the emergence place from the underworld] in the plaza. Within the feminine dark interior, the plaza-space configuration was repeated with the human activity area around a nansipu, the earth floor under and the woven-basket roof above, representing the sky. The connecting ladder made of tall spruce or pine trees stood in the middle near the nansipu. Everything was organized to remind us constantly of the primary connections with the earth, sky, other life forms and the cosmic movement.

It is pure supposition that centuries ago the hole in the floor of the cave at our site might have been created as a symbolic reminder of the emergence place. Nevertheless, it is a beautiful thought for this setting.

As discussed earlier, researchers are looking at rock imagery from the perspective that it was painted or carved by shamans who wished to record their trance experiences. Shamanism is the oldest of humankind's belief systems, and caves played an important part in shamanic practices throughout the world. The shaman's ability to travel to other dimensions, while in an altered state of consciousness, could be enhanced by physical characteristics of the landscape that were looked upon as metaphoric openings to the upper and lower worlds. It is conceivable that the cave at our site may have been the location for a shaman's vision quest. The features found in the cave also fit with shamanism's multi-component belief system and suggest symbolic openings to the worlds above and below: the beautifully sculpted portal, the enhanced opening to the sky, the stone passageway deep into the earth, and the narrow passageway through the split in the boulders at the rear of the cave.

There are other elements found at this site which support the notion that shamanistic ritual took place here. A ring of stones, for example, is believed to generate power and is known to be a place that would enhance a shaman's vision quest. An altered state of consciousness could be induced by a number of conditions, including rhythmic drumming or chanting. Throughout the American Southwest, however, shamans used parts of the Datura plant as an hallucinatory to evoke a trance state. All parts of the plant are potentially poisonous if not used properly, but shamans understood the properties of plants. Shamans were healers, and Datura also was known to be used as an anesthetic during surgery and to prevent miscarriage. The plant is often seen at sacred sites in the Southwest and continues to grow here in all its splendor—a divine essence of an ancient time. Its magic, deep-green carpet covers the south slope of the boulder outcrop in the summer. The long ivory trumpets rise skyward to salute the sun, heralding a new dawn and a new earth spirit.

Lithic (stone) tools include a grinding stone, *metate*, and an assortment of handstones, *manos*, adjacent and beneath the metate at top of photo. In the center are lithic tools— hammerstones, scrapers, chisels, grinding stones, and below, projectile points.

Creamy white quartz is also found scattered about the site. Quartz is charged with symbolic power, and shamans around the world believe it can magnify psychic energy and healing power. By breaking up quartz, a shaman believed that the power contained within the stone would be released, entering his/her body. I stood transfixed and stared at a dirt-encrusted quartz crystal lying on the desert floor. Exotic mineral specimens such as these were used in ceremonies and also as personal fetishes. We chose chunks of creamy white quartz from our site to outline the seven-circuit walking labyrinth that we created. The labyrinth repeats the design of ancient circular symbols of emergence and rebirth found engraved on rocks south of Oraibi and near Shipaulovi on the Hopi mesas. The remains of a fourteenth-century Hohokam building at Casa Grande, Arizona, have the same circular

The ring of rocks that now encircles a palo verde tree might have been associated with shamanic vision quests centuries ago.

symbol carved on an interior adobe wall. My research on the ancient design revealed that hundreds of the same symbol, outlined in stone, were created centuries ago along the coasts of Finland and Sweden, the land of my ancestors, which supports the notion of human universals.

Who were the people who had a propensity for stone sculpture, deliberately carving their messages in stone? Millennia ago, the first people that traversed central Arizona were the Paleo-Indians who followed the migratory paths of large animals, such as mammoths and bison. As the climate shifted and large animals were no longer plentiful, the Clovis hunting culture gave way to sparse populations of semi-nomadic hunters and gatherers who visited this location during the Archaic period in the Southwest from 8400 B.C. to A.D. 200. Their material cultural remains—potsherds, projectile points, stone chippings, and small lithic tools—have

been uncovered by rivulets of water running down the gentle slope after a downpour of rain. Along the arroyo, the rush of water occasionally unearths a hammerstone, beveled adze, or a scraper with a serrated edge.

The last people to visit the site were the Hohokam. Broken pieces of their pottery with painted designs confirm that they were here. Their once-thriving culture inhabited the riverine areas of the Salt and Gila Rivers in central Arizona. By A.D. 1200, the people had created over six hundred miles of canals using small stone tools. Then they gradually migrated into the Sonoran Desert foothills. Wild food was plentiful and water flowed in nearby Cave Creek. The people were called Hohokam by the O'odham people in Arizona, a word from their Piman language that means "all used up." The end dates of the Hohokam tradition are not well

Indentations in the stone might have been created while grinding shell-encased wild food with a lithic tool, but sometimes, stone was finely ground for ritual purposes. A three-dimensional circle is carved on top of the boulder.

established, but between 1350 and 1450, most sites were abandoned. In the thirteenth century, drought conditions prevailed, and floods between 1356 and 1382 destroyed the vast canal system. The enormous fluctuations of a desert environment and the pressures of an enlarged population, combined with a limitation of resources, are believed to have been major factors in the abandonments centuries ago. The premise set forth by some archaeologists, however, asserts it was more than that: The resources were all used up.

The migrations continued.

"Spirit Fire to the Mountain God," by photographer Edward S. Curtis, circa 1904. —From the Empie collection

Following pages: The seven-path labyrinth lined with creamy white quartz is an ancient symbol engraved on rocks near Oraibi and Shipaulovi on the Hopi mesas. The same symbol appears on an interior adobe wall in the remains of a fourteenth-century Hohokam structure at Casa Grande, Arizona.

My Sacred Garden

Sacred Datura, a glorious plant
as old as the Sanskrit word, dhattura.
Trumpetlike blooms, perfect as my Lilly.
Thorny seed pods, protected by God's design.
Broad green leaves, bold and shiny,
soaking up the sun's rays, shading a small rabbit.
Receiving Earth's energies and giving back.

"They don't belong here, not here,"
Jamestown settlers said.
They're weeds, Jimsonweeds.
Methodically, resolutely,
they ripped their roots from the ground.
They don't belong here,
Not here.

Earth's sacred plant arises each year,
hugging the hillside, blooming brightly
a divine essence of an ancient time.
Long, ivory trumpets raise skyward
moving in concert with the soft caress of the wind,
saluting the sun,
heralding a new Earth spirit.

The difference is human perspective.
They belong there. Here,
where their roots have been recreating for centuries,
where we can hear their ancient song.

Come, listen, to my sacred garden.

Minding A Sacred Place
The Empie Petroglyph Site

We walk the same paths as the ancient people. We sleep beneath the same boulders. We hear their whispers on the wind. The sacred site is a place of great spirit and presence that neither time nor event has altered. For a thousand years, the rocks did not speak to anyone—and then they confided in us. We give voice, at this time, in this place, to the ancient messages that are reappearing after centuries of silence. And we will always ponder the questions: Why us? Why now?

Thirty years ago, Bill and I began a journey that directed us to the outcrop of boulders. Had we known then that this is a sacred place, we would not have contemplated building the Boulder House. But that is not how the story unfolds. Following a path that was created for us, we came upon the "beautiful pile of boulders" and sensed a profound spirit of place. Only later would we learn that our emotional encounter, a moment we shall forever remember, was prompted by more than the impressive size of the boulders. Now we see them from another perspective—not just as objects in the landscape—but also as witness to time past, present, and future.

Centuries ago, people abandoned this site, leaving behind not only their stone implements, but also an incredible story that unfolded to reveal an ancient cosmology. The people are gone, the storytellers are gone, but their history survives in metaphoric symbols that embody their beliefs. Within the boulders, they left symbols charged with significance: circle and spiral petroglyphs that interact with sundaggers to mark calendrical events, such as solstice and equinox, and vulva

symbols that were carved in granitic stone in veneration of an Earth Mother. We remain in awe that we are the first persons since the Hohokam to observe and record the sun's interaction with rock symbols.

What does it mean to live on a sacred site? It is an illuminating experience— and an awakening to the aspects of place: a sense of place, the spirit of place, and the power of place. A site's intrinsic power may be inexpressible and abstract, but it is perceived and acknowledged within the heart and soul. A reverence for Nature is the heritage of all people, and certain elements of the natural landscape are still considered by native people to be sacred. Depending on the physical geography, these include natural rock formations or stones as shrines, caves, springs, mountains, or trees. Natural sites that have an inherent spirit may be used for specific purposes, such as healing, purification, pilgrimage, and vision questing. There are

A dust storm moves across the high Sonoran Desert.

Coyote survives
  in spite of bounties
    poisons, development
Whatever means
    humans have taken
  to eradicate this creature.

Coyote survives
    with certainty.

  Raising her head
    from the waterhole
looking us straight in the eye
  She walks away
  a parting glance
    over her shoulder.

Comfortable in her surroundings
    forever at home.

Acknowledgments

Minding a Sacred Place is dedicated to our grandchildren who have climbed the walls of their "Rock House." They nourish the child in us and share our excitement in what Nature offers. We hope to enrich their lives by telling our story about this sacred place and the architecture that was created here.

I am indebted to the scholars and authors whose published material validated my thoughts and inspired me to write about a sacred place. The encourage-

ment I have given my family over the years returned full circle with their support for my goal of telling this story— my husband, Bill Empie, my daughters and their husbands, Scot and Kristen Lindskog Jarvis, Chris and Leslie Lindskog Burrows, and Thierry and Lauren Lindskog Blanc.

We thank Marguerette and Augustus W. Empie for sharing their knowledge of flora and fauna and their loving care of this place; my parents, Lillian and Daniel Sundquist, who allowed me freedom in Nature; Jean Lipman, a remarkable role model and support person; Charles F. Johnson, designer of the Boulder House; and Stanley Marcus, for his inspiration and support of our dwelling as "among the most exciting."

The Empie Petroglyph Site AZ U: 1: 165 (ASM) was placed on the National Register of Historic Places in 1998. We thank the knowledgeable professionals who submitted site evaluations in support of the nomination: Larry Loendorf, Chris Loendorf, Bruce Masse, Todd Bostwick, and Grace S. Schoonover, past president, Desert Foothills Chapter, Arizona Archaeological Society. We appreciate the support of a brilliant and affable editor, Robin Beaver; talented book designer David Alcorn; and K. J. Schroeder, consulting archaeologist. My harshest critic, Bertou, listened to chapters read aloud for countless hours, his ears pointed in attention and paws crossed. I knew there was a problem in the text if he went to sleep.

Living with Nature and natural architecture on a sacred site is for us the ultimate experience. We honor this place for the gifts to our spiritual and physical well being and for giving us this story. We honor our guides and spirit helpers, past and present. We are humbled that after many centuries, we were the chosen ones to make these observations and to share our findings through this publication.

—**Sunnie Empie**

Few people have the opportunity and privilege for a long-time relationship with a sacred place and to witness and capture on film, over a period of twenty-five years, the varying changes in landscape, weather, and the revelations of the site that have made possible the varied and profound selection of images for *Minding a Sacred Place.*

—**Photographer Hart W. Empie**

Photo credits:

Charles F. Johnson	pp. 30, 31, 32, 36, 37, 45, 57;
John Brinkman Photography	p. 184 and jacket;
Drawing by Jessica Jarvis	p. 118.

Permissions granted by Beacon Press for excerpts from *The Sacred Hoop: Recovering the Feminine in American Indian Traditions* by Paula Gunn Allen; *Architectural Digest* for quote by Joseph Giovannini.

Following page: A handprint petroglyph appears just above the darkened concave circle in the center of the monolith that we call God's hand. By painting or pecking the outline of their hands on stone, native people created an intimate relationship with the spirit of the rock.

Publications in which the Boulder House is referenced:

BOOKS

Architectural Digest, eds. *The AD 100 Architects: An Exclusive Guide to the World's Foremost Architects.* 1991, 130-31.

Baca, Elmo, and Suzanne Deats. *Santa Fe Design.* Lincolnwood, Illinois: Publications International, Limited, 1990, 5, 90, 107, 155.

Ebert, Wolfgang M. *Wahnsinn Wohnen.* Koln, Germany: im Rudolf Muller Verlag, 1987, 74-91.

Emmerling, Mary. *American Country West.* New York: Clarkson N. Potter, Inc., 1985, 78-83.

Empie, Sunnie. "The Empie Petroglyph Site," *McDowell Mountains Archaeological Symposium.* Publication of Papers Presented March 20, 1999. Ed. K. J. Schroeder. Scottsdale: Roadrunner Publications in Anthropology 10, 1999, 251-260. Photographs Hart W. Empie.

Hess, Alan. *Hyperwest: American Residential Architecture on the Edge.* London: Thames & Hudson, 1996, 26-29.

Lichfield, Lord, ed. "The best house in America." Courvoisier's *Book of the Best.* Topsfield, Massachusetts: Salem House Publishers, 1986, 239.

Mather, Christine, and Sharon Woods. *Santa Fe Style.* New York: Rizzoli International Publications, Inc., 1986, 224-29.

Pearson, David. *The Natural House.* New York: Simon and Schuster/Fireside; London, England: Conran Octopus Limited, 1989, Photos cover, frontispiece, 33-35, 147.

Romero, Orlando, and David Larkin. *Adobe: Building and Living with Earth.* Boston: Houghton Mifflin, 1994, 214-28.

Seth, Sandra, and Laurel Seth. *Adobe! Homes and Interiors of Taos, Santa Fe and The Southwest.* Stamford: Architectural Book Publishing Company, 1988, 260-61, 264-68.

MAGAZINES

Bill, Andrew, ed. "The Carefree Life." *Town and Country*, Dec. 1987. Sandy Granville Sheehy, text; Robert Phillips, photographer.

Cheek, Lawrence W. "Arizona's Architecture." *Arizona Highways,* May 1984. Photo by Hart W. Empie.

Cheek, Lawrence W. "Cave Creek and Carefree." *Arizona Highways*, Sept. 1989. Frontispiece photo.

The saguaro cactus, *Cereus giganteus,* wears a cluster of creamy white flowers in late spring.

Bibliography

Allen, Paula Gunn. *The Sacred Hoop: Recovering the Feminine in American Indian Traditions.* Boston: Beacon Press, 1992.

Aveni, Anthony F., ed. *Native American Astronomy.* Austin: University of Texas Press, 1977.

Ayers, James E. "A Prehistoric Farm Site Near Cave Creek, Arizona." *The Kiva* 32 (1967): 106-11.

Bahn, Paul G. *Prehistoric Art.* Cambridge: Cambridge University Press, 1998.

Bean, Lowell John, ed. *California Indian Shamanism.* Menlo Park, Calif.: Ballena Press, 1992.

Beck, Peggy V., Anna Lee Walters, and Nia Francisco. *The Sacred: Ways of Knowledge, Sources of Life.* Tsaile, Ariz.: Navajo Community College Press, 1992.

Benson, Arlene, and Tom Hoskinson, eds. *Earth and Sky: Papers from the Northridge Conference on Archaeoastronomy.* Thousand Oaks, Calif.: Slo'w Press, 1985.

Calvin, William H. *How the Shaman Stole the Moon: In Search of Ancient Prophet-Scientists from Stonehenge to the Grand Canyon.* New York: Bantam Books, 1991.

Campbell, Joseph. *Primitive Mythology: The Masks of God.* New York: Penguin, 1959, 1969.

Camphausen, Rufus C. *The Yoni: Sacred Symbol of Female Creative Power.* Rochester, Vermont: Inner Traditions, 1996.

Capps, Walter Holden. *Seeing with a Native Eye: Essays on Native American Religion.* New York: Harper & Row, 1976.

Carlson, John B. "America's Ancient Skywatchers." *National Geographic* 177, No. 3, (1990): 76-107.

Carlson, John B., and W. James Judge. *Astronomy and Ceremony in the Prehistoric Southwest.* Albuquerque: Maxwell Museum of Anthropology, University of New Mexico, 1983.

Clottes, Jean, and David Lewis-Williams. *The Shamans of Prehistory: Trance and Magic in the Painted Caves.* New York: Harry N. Abrams, 1998.

Cordell, Linda S. *Archaeology of the Southwest.* 2d ed. Boulder, Colo.: Academic Press, Inc., 1997.

Crotty, Helen K. "The Rock Art Recording Field School of the Archaeological Society of New Mexico." *The First 100 Years: Papers in Honor of the State and Local Archaeological Societies of New Mexico*, 113. Albuquerque: The Archaeological Society of New Mexico, 2000.

Courlander, Harold. *The Fourth World of the Hopis.* Albuquerque: University of New Mexico Press, 1992.

Barrel cactus, *Ferocactus,* wears a golden crown of spring blossoms.

Devereux, Paul. *Earth Memory: Sacred Sites—Doorways into Earth's Mysteries.* St. Paul: Llewellyn Publications, 1992.

Downum, Christian E., and Todd W. Bostwick. *Archaeology of the Pueblo Grande Platform Mound and Surrounding Features*, Phoenix: Pueblo Grande Museum Anthropological Papers No. 1, 1993.

Eliade, Mircea. *Shamanism: Archaic Techniques of Ecstasy.* Bollingen Series LXXVI, Princeton University Press, 1972.

Ellis, Florence H., and Hammack, Laurens. "The Inner Sanctum of Feather Cave, A Mogollon Sun and Earth Shrine Linking Mexico and the Southwest." *American Antiquity* xxxiii (1968): 25-44.

Fewkes, Jesse Walter. *Archeological Expedition to Arizona in 1895.* Bureau of American Ethnology 17th Annual Report 1895-1896, Part II. Reprinted Glorieta, N. M.: Rio Grande Press, Inc., 1971.

Fowles, John. *The Enigma of Stonehenge.* New York: Summit Books, 1980.

Gadon, Elinor W. *The Once and Future Goddess: A Symbol for Our Time.* New York: HarperCollins, 1989.

Giedion, S. *The Eternal Present I: The Beginnings of Art.* Princeton: Princeton University Press, 1964.

Gimbutas, Marija. *The Language of the Goddess: Unearthing the Hidden Symbols of Western Civilization.* New York: HarperCollins, 1989.

Gladwin, Harold S., Emil W. Haury, E. B. Sayles, and Nora Gladwin. *Excavations at Snaketown. Material Culture.* Tucson: University of Arizona Press, 1975.

Hadingham, Evan. *Early Man and the Cosmos.* New York: Walker and Company, 1984.

Harner, Michael. *The Way of the Shaman.* San Francisco: HarperSan Francisco, 1990.

Haury, Emil W. *The Hohokam, Desert Farmers and Craftsmen: Excavations* at *Snaketown 1964-65*, 1975.

———. *Prehistory of the American Southwest.* Edited by J. J. Reid and D. E. Doyel. Tucson: University of Arizona Press, 1986.

Hawkins, Gerald S., and John B. White. *Stonehenge Decoded.* New York: Dell Publishing Co., 1966.

Hedges, Ken, ed. *Rock Art Papers 2.* San Diego: San Diego Museum Papers No. 18, 1985.

———. *Rock Art Papers 5.* San Diego: San Diego Museum Papers No. 23, 1987.

———. *Rock Art Papers 7.* San Diego: San Diego Museum Papers No. 26, 1990.

Henderson, T. K., and J. B. Rodgers. *Archaeological Investigations in the Cave Creek Area, Maricopa County, South-Central Arizona.* Arizona State University Anthropological Research Papers No. 17.

Hieb, Louis A. "Hopi World View." *Handbook of North American Indians*: 577-80.

Krupp, E. C. *In Search of Ancient Astronomies.* New York: McGraw Hill, 1979.

———. *Echoes of the Ancient Skies, the Astronomy of Lost Civilizations.* New York: Harper & Row, 1983.

———. *Skywatchers, Shamans and Kings: Astronomy and the Archaeology of Power.* New York: John Wiley & Sons, 1997.

MacMahon, J. A. *Deserts.* The Audubon Society Nature Guide. New York: Alfred A. Knopf, 1985.

Malville, J. McKim, and Claudia Putnam. *Prehistoric Astronomy in the Southwest.* rev. ed. Boulder, Colo.: Johnson Books, 1993.

Mann, A. T. *Sacred Architecture.* Rockport, Me.: Element, 1993.

McCluskey, Stephen C. "The Astronomy of the Hopi Indians." *Journal for the History of Astronomy* viii (1977): 174-95.

———. "Calendars and Symbolism: Functions of Observation in Hopi Astronomy." *Archaeoastronomy* 15 (JHA, xxi) (1990): S1-S8.

McCoy, Ron. *Archaeoastronomy: Skywatching in the Native American Southwest.* Flagstaff, Arizona: Museum of Northern Arizona Press, 1992.

McGowan, Charlotte. *Ceremonial Fertility Sites in Southern California.* San Diego: San Diego Museum of Man Museum Papers No. 14, 1982.

McGregor, John C. *Southwestern Archaeology.* 2d ed. Urbana: University of Illinois Press, Illini Books edition, 1982.

Metzner, Ralph. *The Well of Remembrance: Rediscovering the Earth Wisdom Myths of Northern Europe.* Boston: Shambhala, 1994.

Michell, John. *Secrets of the Stones: The Story of Astro-Archaeology.* New York: Penguin Books, 1977.

Nequatewa, Edmund. *Truth of a Hopi: Stories Relating to the Origin, Myths, and Clan Histories of the Hopi.* Flagstaff: Northland Publishing with Museum of Northern Arizona, 1967.

Noble, David Grant, ed. *The Hohokam: Ancient People of the Desert.* Santa Fe: School of American Research, 1991.

———. *New Light on Chaco Canyon.* Santa Fe: School of American Research Press, 1984.

Ortiz, Alfonso. *Handbook of North American Indians, Southwest*, Vol. 9. Washington D. C.: Smithsonian Institution Press, 1979.

Purce, Jill. *The Mystic Spiral: Journey of the Soul*. London: Thames & Hudson, 1974.

Reid, Jefferson, and Stephanie Whittlesey. *The Archaeology of Ancient Arizona*. Tucson: The University of Arizona Press, 1997.

Schaafsma, Polly. *Indian Rock Art of the Southwest*. Santa Fe: School of American Research, 1980.

————. *Rock Art in New Mexico*. Santa Fe: Museum of New Mexico Press, 1992.

Scully, Vincent. *Pueblo: Mountain, Village, Dance*. New York: Viking Press, 1975.

————. "Mankind and the Earth in American and Europe." *The Ancient Americas: Art from Sacred Landscapes*. Edited by Richard F. Townsend, 71-82. Chicago: The Art Institute of Chicago, 1992.

Stevenson, Matilda Coxe. *The Zuni Indians: Their Mythology, Esoteric Fraternities, & Ceremonies*. 23rd Report of the Bureau of American Ethnology, 1904. Reprinted 1970, Glorieta, N. M.: Rio Grande Press, Inc., 1970.

Streep, Peg. *Sanctuaries of the Goddess: The Sacred Landscapes and Objects*. Boston: Bulfinch Press, 1994.

Swan, James A. *Sacred Places*: *How the Living Earth Seeks Our Friendship*. Santa Fe: Bear & Co., 1990.

Swentzell, Rina. "An Understated Sacredness." MASS*: Journal of the School of Architecture and Planning*. Albuquerque: University of New Mexico (Fall 1985).

————. "Remembering Tewa Pueblo Houses and Spaces." *Native Peoples* (Winter 1990): 6-12.

Vastokas, Joan M. and Romas K. Vastokas. *Sacred Art of the Algonkians: A Study of the Peterborough Petroglyphs*. Peterborough, Ontario: Mansard Press, 1973.

Waters, Frank. *Book of the Hopi*. Middlesex, England: Penguin Books, 1983.

Whitley, David S. and Lawrence L. Loendorf, eds. *New Light on Old Art: Recent Advances in Hunter Gatherer Rock Art Research*. Los Angeles: Institute of Archaeology, University of California, 1994.

Whitley, David S., ed. *A Guide to Rock Art Sites: Southern California and Southern Nevada*. Missoula, Mont.: Mountain Press Publishing Company, 1996.

————. "Reading the Minds of Rock Artist." *American Archaeology* (1997) Vol. 1, No. 3: 19-23.

————. "Ethnography and Rock Art in the Far West: Some Archaeological Implications."

New Light on Old Art: Recent Advances in Hunter Gatherer Rock Art Research, 81-93. Institute of Archaeology, University of California, Los Angeles, 1994.

———. "Shamanism, Natural Modeling and the Rock Art of Far Western North American Hunter-Gatherers." *Shamanism and Rock Art in North America*. Edited by Solveig A. Turpin, 1-43. San Antonio, Tex.: Rock Art Foundation, Inc., 1994.

Williamson, Ray A. *Living the Sky—the Cosmos of the American Indian*. Norman: University of Oklahoma Press, 1984.

Zeilik, Michael. "Sun Shrines and Sun Symbols in the U.S. Southwest." *Archaeoastronomy* 9 (Supplement to the Journal for the History of Astronomy, No. 9) (1985): S86-96.

———. "The Ethnoastronomy of the Historic Pueblos, I: Calendrical Sun Watching." *Archaeoastronomy* 8 (Journal for the History of Astronomy, xvi) (1985): S1-S24.

———. "A Reassessment of the Fajada Butte Solar Marker." *Archaeoastronomy* 9 (Journal for the History of Astronomy, xvi) (1985): S69-S85.

———. "The Sunwatchers of Chaco Canyon." *Griffith Observer* 47, No. 6 (June 1983): 2-20.

Index

The design and production of this book was accomplished with PageMaker 6.5 software on Power Mac G4 computers at Alcorn Publication Design, Red Bluff, California and output on a Linotype-Hell imagesetter at CS Graphics in Singapore.

The family of type used throughout this book is Adobe Garamond in its roman, italic, bold, and bold italic forms.

The book was printed on 170 gsm Leykam Matt using a Heidelberg Speedmaster press, Smyth sewn and case bound in Singapore.

Published in the United States of America.